NAPLES
POMPEII, CAPRI, SORRENTO AND THE AMALFI COAST
in your pocket

TEXT: MELISSA SHALES

PHOTOGRAPH CREDITS
Photos supplied by The Travel Library:
Stuart Black title page, 65, 66, 79, 81, 83, 88, 93, 97, 102; David Carter 49, 53, 63, 80, 80-81, 107, 109, 115, 120; Philip Enticknap 77; Jeremy Gould 61, 69(b); Chris North 51; R Richardson front cover, 55, 59; Jonathan Smith back cover, 5, 7, 8, 12(t), 19, 20, 21, 22, 23, 24, 25(t,b), 26, 27, 28, 29, 31, 32, 34, 35, 37, 38, 39, 40, 41, 43, 44, 46, 54, 60, 62, 67, 68, 69(t), 70, 71, 73, 74, 75, 85, 87, 94, 105, 111, 125; Peter Terry 86; John Welburn 99.
Other Photos:
Museo Nazionale di Capodimonte, Naples/Bridgeman Art Library 10-11, Museo Nazionale di San Martino/Roger-Viollet, Paris/Bridgeman Art Library 12(b), Casa Goldoni, Venice, Italy/Bridgeman Art Library 17.

Front cover: Amalfi, with the Cathedral dome;
back cover: looking across the Bay of Naples to Vesuvius;
title page: view of Maiori, Cape Orso and the Gulf of Salerno from Villa Rufolo, Ravello.

MANUFACTURE FRANÇAISE DES PNEUMATIQUES MICHELIN
Place des Carmes-Déchaux – 63000 Clermont-Ferrand (France)
© Michelin et Cie. Propriétaires-Éditeurs 2000
Dépôt légal Jan 2000 – ISBN 2-06-653301-7 – ISSN 1272-1689
No part of this publication may be reproduced in any form
without the prior permission of the publisher.
Printed in Spain 1-00

MICHELIN TYRE PLC
Travel Publications
The Edward Hyde Building
38 Clarendon Road
WATFORD Herts WD1 1SX - UK
☎ (01923) 415000

MICHELIN TRAVEL PUBLICATIONS
Editorial Department
One Parkway South
GREENVILLE, SC 29615
☎ 1-800 423-0485

CONTENTS

INTRODUCTION

'Anyone can be forgiven for losing his mind in Naples.'
Goethe, Feb 1787

After the fall of Troy, Odysseus, that heroic but appalling navigator, sailed home to Greece, absent-mindedly circumnavigating the Mediterranean for seven years en route! At the *Li Galli* islands, off the Amalfi coast, he met the Sirens who tried to lure him onto the rocks with their sweet song. Strong-minded enough to resist, he journeyed on. The Siren Parthenope was washed up on the mainland shore, where she founded a new town – or so the legend goes.

A few hundred years later, in the 6C BC, Greek settlers arrived, named this settlement *Palaeopolis* (Old Town) and built a new one next door. In a moment of sheer inspiration, they named it *Neapolis* (New Town). So Naples was born.

From these romantic beginnings has grown one of the most exciting, dramatic and controversial cities on the Mediterranean, set precariously in what is, without question, one of Europe's most beautiful bays, overshadowed by an angry and very active volcano.

Sorrento, across the bay, and the off-shore islands of Capri and Ischia have ranked amongst Europe's top holiday resorts for the last 2 000 years. Pompeii became an essential stop on the Grand Tour in the mid-18C. Naples itself has had a more chequered past. Over the last few decades, far too many people have ignored the city centre, only making a short dash to the Archaeological Museum, frightened by stories of desperate poverty and crime.

Yes, Naples does have terrible poverty. Yes, Naples is the home of the Camorra, a home-grown variant of the Mafia. And yes, there is some street crime. This is nonetheless a major international city. The dirt, the poverty and the street crime are no greater than in Paris or London. Enormous efforts have been made in recent years to clean up and restore the historic city centre. Modern Naples is frenetic, noisy, compelling, and very, very beautiful, filled with fascinating historic sights, wonderful walks and delicious food. What more can you ask?

Via San Gregorio Armeno, a charming street lined by shops and workshops selling presepi (see p.106)

GEOGRAPHY

Naples, a rapidly growing conurbation of nearly 2 million people, is the economic powerhouse of southern Italy. Stripped of its political status by unification (although it is still capital of the region of Campania), the city remains a busy **port**, while nearby Castellammare di Stabia is home to Italy's main **naval base**.

Vesuvius looms over the Bay of Naples.

The roughly semi-circular **Bay of Naples** forms one of Europe's finest natural harbours. Fishing has always been important here, and since the first Greeks started trading 2 500 years ago, the Neapolitans have often looked for their wealth to the distant shores of their trading partners rather than to the rest of Italy.

Potentially the single most important geographic feature of the region is the one that most locals try hardest to ignore. **Mount Vesuvius** is the visible manifestation of a far larger and highly active volcanic area which covers almost the whole of the bay. Its looming presence threatens the very existence of Naples but paradoxically it also provides its lifeblood. The volcanic earth is immensely fertile, allowing intensive farming throughout much of the bay area. The volcano is also the linchpin of the booming tourist trade that has become the region's single most important moneyspinner.

HISTORY

The Early Years

Archaeologically speaking, the earliest known settlement within the curve of the bay was in the 8C BC. Over the next 200 years, Greek colonists founded several towns along the coast, including Pompeii, Herculaneum, Sorrento and Naples itself. In 474 BC they halted the relentless advance of the Etruscans and forced them out of southern Italy.

The following century brought a new conqueror, however, as the Samnite peoples spread south from the Apennines. Yet although the Samnites nominally took control, the prosperous coastal trading towns still maintained a largely Greek lifestyle, and Greek remained the language of choice even during much of the Roman period. The towns thrived on trade and, in later years, as a tourist destination for the patrician elite from Rome.

The Roman Empire

From 343-290 BC, Rome began its ferocious conquest of the rest of Italy. In 328 BC the Samnite rulers of Naples were forced to ally themselves with the Empire, although they did not come under direct control until 89 BC, when the people of Campania were formally granted Roman citizenship.

Life went on much as before until AD 79, when the massive eruption of Vesuvius buried Pompeii and Herculaneum under 6m (19ft) of ash, rock and stone (*see* p.60). Naples itself survived, and continued to flourish. Within 200 years, Christianity was growing to outstrip the old religions, but the onset of the Barbarian invasions began to cripple the Roman Empire. In AD 330 Constantine transferred his power base to Constantinople and the Western Empire became a sad and second-rate affair. It ended officially in 476, when the last emperor, Romulus Augustulus, was deposed and imprisoned in the *Castrum Lucullanum* (where the Castel dell'Ovo now stands).

The ruins of the Temple of Apollo, part of the thriving Roman city of Pompeii.

The Byzantine Era

In 540 the Byzantine **Emperor Justinian** began a bloody reconquest of Italy, with many of the most ferocious battles being fought in Campania. The coastal cities were unharmed and, in 553, formally switched allegiance to Byzantium.

The next threat came from the Germanic **Lombards** who crossed into northern Italy in 568, eventually besieging Naples in 600. The Neapolitans managed to beat them off and a complex pattern of power developed. The Lombard chiefs, who had overrun northern Italy, ruled much of the interior in the south, while the coastal areas were defended by semi-independent Byzantine dukes. Naples declared itself independent in 763, while along the coast Amalfi became an autonomous republic in 839, still under the protection of Byzantium, finally becoming a Duchy in 958.

The greatest danger to the region came in the late 9C. In 827 Sicily was invaded by **Saracens**, who used it as a springboard from which to attack the mainland. It was 902 before they were eventually defeated at the **Battle of Garigliano**.

The Angevins

In a spirit of Christian (or rather, anti-Muslim) brotherhood, the Duke of Naples granted a tract of land around Aversa to the Normans in 1030. After recapturing Sicily from the Saracens, the ungrateful Normans turned their attentions to the rest of southern Italy, receiving papal blessing for their conquest in 1059. In 1130 **Roger II of Anjou** was crowned King of Sicily. In 1139 the Duchy of Naples itself was ceded to Norman rule, under a new dynasty of Angevin kings.

BACKGROUND

The Angevin reign was patchy and fraught with disaster. In 1189 King William II died without an heir and the kingdom became caught up in a much greater power struggle between the Pope, Anti-Pope, Holy Roman Emperor and various pretenders to the Imperial crown. In 1266 **Charles of Anjou** eventually won the Battle of Benevento and with it, the crown of Sicily, making Naples his capital. In 1282 the Angevins lost the island of Sicily to the Aragonese. The mainland kingdom now became known as Naples.

The beginning of the 14C saw the early flowering of the **Renaissance** in Naples, as elsewhere, with King **Robert the Wise** attracting such great men of letters and art as Boccaccio, Petrarch and Giotto to the city. On his death in 1343, under the less assured rule of his granddaughter, Giovanna I, the kingdom was gradually torn to pieces by civil strife and rival claims to the throne.

A Spanish Kingdom

In 1421 the last of the Angevin monarchs, Joan II, left her throne to **Alfonso V** of Aragon, who reunited Naples and Sicily, ruled with harsh and ruthless skill, and restored a degree of wealth and prestige to the country. In 1503 the kingdom finally lost its independence and became a colony of Spain, ruled with an iron fist by a Viceroy.

The mid-17C spelt disaster for the city. As Naples burst out beyond its walls, to create new districts along the seafront and around modern Via Toledo and Chiaia, the Spanish treated the territory as a cash cow, taxing heavily and even press-ganging a reluctant population into military service. Hounded by merciless feudal barons, driven by poverty and appalling living conditions, thousands of peasants left the villages of the rural south for the only marginally safer Naples.

Worse was to come. In 1631 Vesuvius erupted, although the city itself was spared.

View of Naples depicting the Aragonese fleet re-entering the port after the Battle of Ischia in 1442, by Francesco Rosselli (Palazzo e Galleria Nazionale di Capodimonte, Naples).

In 1647 the people of Naples rioted in a vain attempt to declare a republic. The discontent and uprising spread throughout the south but was mercilessly crushed by the Spanish, who by the time the unrest was finally quashed had killed over 18 000 people. In 1656 an outbreak of plague wiped out a third of the city's population and in

The Arco di Trionfo di Alfonso, Castel Nuovo, was built in honour of Alfonso V and depicts his entry into Naples in 1443.

1688 most of the old city was destroyed by a horrific earthquake.

Campania's next incarnation was decided far beyond its borders when the death of Charles II in 1700 led to the **War of the Spanish Succession**. In 1713, under the terms of the Peace of Utrecht, control of all Italy passed to the Austrian Habsburgs. In 1734, however, the Spanish regained control. Naples became an independent kingdom once more, under the rule of Bourbon King **Charles III**, who introduced some much-needed reforms, started the excavation of Pompeii, and built the magnificent Teatro San Carlo, the Archaeological Museum, and Capodimonte and Caserta Palaces.

In 1793 the British Admiral of the Fleet, Lord Nelson, visited Naples and first met his great love, Lady Emma Hamilton, wife of the British ambassador.

The marketplace in Naples during the plague of 1656, by Carlo Cappola (Museo Nazionale di San Martino, Naples).

Napoleon

The rule of the Bourbons in Naples came to an end in 1799, with Napoleon's defeat of **King Ferdinand**. The Neapolitans promptly set up a Republic, which survived only six months before Ferdinand returned and, with the assistance of the vicious Cardinal Ruffo, suppressed it, laying waste the city and executing the ringleaders.

In 1806 Ferdinand fled again, in the face of Napoleon's advance. Napoleon bestowed the crown on his brother, Joseph. It was then inherited by Joachim Murat (Napoleon's brother-in-law), who reigned briefly as King Joachim. In 1815, with the fall of Napoleon, Ferdinand was again restored to the throne of the renamed **Kingdom of the Two Sicilies**. Murat was executed.

Unification

In 1820 the first, ineffectual, republican **riots** erupted in Naples, led by a secret masonic society, the Carbonari. Others followed across Italy, the driving force towards nationalism coming from the new middle class intelligentsia. In 1847 the Sicilians forced **Ferdinand II** to give them a constitution; their success inspired others further north. By 1849, however, most of the fuss was over, with little to show for it.

The next real action originated in Piedmont, in the north, under the control of **King Vittorio Emanuele II**, his prime minister, Camillo de Cavour, and his commander-in-chief, **Giuseppe Garibaldi**, who were determined to drive the Austrians from Italian soil and who set about manufacturing a war, which eventually broke out in 1859. The peace treaty gave Piedmont most of northern Italy, while the Pope controlled a central federation and the south remained intact. Early in 1860 Garibaldi took a volunteer force to Sicily to support a local rebellion. He succeeded rather too well, and by 7 September was in control of the whole of southern Italy and marching towards Rome. Cavour hurriedly sent the Piedmontese army south to link up. On the 8 November 1860 Garibaldi declared Vittorio Emanuele king of a united Italy.

The Twentieth Century

Life in Naples reverted to the normal mix of grandiose planning at the upper end of the social spectrum, and dire poverty at the lower. After a serious outbreak of cholera in 1884, thousands emigrated to the United States.

Italy entered the First World War in 1915 on the side of the Allies, suffered heavy defeats and massive casualties and was left in economic and social chaos, ripe for the iron hand of the Fascists. In October 1922 **Mussolini** and his 'black shirts' marched on Rome, where the king asked him to form a government.

The next decade saw a dramatic improvement in the economy, along with a vast proliferation of corruption and a total denial of all human rights. In 1936 Mussolini signed the Axis pact with Hitler, which was to plunge a largely reluctant Italy into the Second World War.

By 1943 the country was in a desperate state. As the Allies landed, Mussolini was forced to resign. The new premier sued for peace, then re-entered the war on the side of the Allies, who fought a bitter campaign up through Italy, finally liberating the country in May 1944. The previous month, Mussolini had been shot by partisans and hung upside-down from a lamp post in Milan. In 1946 the king abdicated and Italy became a **democratic republic**.

Since then, although dogged by fragmented politics, occasional outbursts of left and right wing terrorism, constant corruption scandals and the veiled threat of the Sicilian Mafia and Neapolitan Camorra, Italy has remained stable, its economy has flourished and it is now a valuable member of the European Union.

In an effort to break the cycle of too many political parties, lame duck administrations and a rapid turnover of government, the electoral method was changed in 1993. Now 75 percent of parliamentary seats are elected on a first-past-the-post system, while the remaining 25 percent are still voted in by proportional representation.

PEOPLE AND CULTURE

North and South

The people of southern Italy are different from the northerners. Physically, they tend to be smaller and darker. Culturally, they have been linked to the north only since 1860 – no time at all in historic terms. Instead, they have been shaped by many and varied influences, from the Greeks to the Romans, Byzantines, Arabs, Normans and Spanish, all of whom have left a mark on local art and architecture, on the diet and even on the tongue. The Neapolitan dialect still contains words borrowed from all these different peoples, mixed into a harshly accented soup that is virtually incomprehensible to the outsider.

People here still think of themselves as Neapolitan first and Italian second. Northern Italians consider the Neapolitans lazy and shiftless; Neapolitans think the northerners uptight and arrogant. The Neapolitans are charming, passionate and volatile, quick to anger and amusement, warm and generous to strangers. Socialising is a far more important part of life than working.

O Sole Mio

Anywhere else but Italy, the artistic and architectural heritage of Naples would be impressive. Here, however, although there are many wonderful buildings and fine paintings, the shadow cast by Tuscany, Venice and Rome is simply too long. Where Naples has shone is in **music and drama**. Most famous of all are those perennial clichés of Italian popular song, *O Sole Mio* and *Santa Lucia*.

Several Neapolitans were instrumental in creating the satirical 16C-17C *Commedia dell'Arte*. Silvio Fiorillo was probably the first to play the abusive, hook-nosed Pulcinella, who transformed himself into the Russian Petrouchka and English Punch. His son, Tiberio Fiorillo, masterminded the first outings of the braggart army captain, Scaramuccia (Scaramouche, meaning 'old fox'). Naples still has a thriving theatrical tradition, balancing political polemic, the avant garde, high drama and popular melodrama, the *sceneggiata*. Cinematically, the region has starred in many Italian and Hollywood movies, but its greatest gift to the screen is undoubtedly Sofia Loren.

Spavento, one of the characters from the Commedia dell'Arte.

Opera was popular in Naples from the early 17C onwards, but it took 50 years to come of age under the pen of Alessandro Scarlatti (1660-1725) who first created the grand operatic formula we know today, with show-off arias separated by recitative (story). In 1737 the magnificent Teatro San Carlo was built (40 years before La Scala in Milan). Over the next 150 years, it was one of the most influential opera houses in the world, with Donizetti, Rossini and Verdi all acting as Artistic Director.

MUST SEE

Museo Archeologico Nazionale★★★ (National Archaeological Museum)

Of any sight in the city, this must be the most important, housing one of the world's greatest collections of **Greco-Roman art★★★**, with the magnificent Farnese collection added to the superbly preserved **mosaics★★** and **frescoes★★★** from Pompeii and Herculaneum.

Castel Nuovo★★

The blackened, brooding bulk of the **Castel Nuovo★★** was built by the Angevins in 1279 to guard the port, and rebuilt by the Spanish in the mid 15C. Its finest feature is the magnificent **Arco di Trionfo di Alfonso★★** at the entrance, with its lavish sculpture praising the exploits of the modest king.

Porto di Santa Lucia★★

Jutting out from the centre of the bay on a tiny islet, effectively now separating the work and play areas of the waterfront, stands one of the most famous sights in Naples, the medieval **Castel dell'Ovo**. The Borgo Marinaro, the old fishing village at its feet, has been transformed into a trendy marina and restaurant area.

Spaccanapoli★★

Old Naples is a small area of narrow streets and alleys almost perpetually shaded by high buildings with iron balconies. Tucked among them are almost a hundred churches, many magnificently decorated. The area is bisected by a long, straight street, a surviving relic of the grid plan of the ancient Greek city, generally known simply as Spaccanapoli (Split-Naples). Running parallel is the lively and characterful **Via Tribunali★**, following the course of the **Decumanus Maximus★★**.

Castel Sant'Elmo and the Certosa di San Martino★★

The castle is imposing and the Monastery of San Martino has a fine art collection, but the real reason to come up here is for the view, which is superb, with Naples and the Bay spread out at your feet.

Palazzo e Galleria Nazionale di Capodimonte★★

Capodimonte is most famous for its frilly, delicate china. These days, however, people flock up the hill to see one of the great palaces and parks of Naples, the Neapolitan national collection of paintings, and, of course, the view.

Interior of the Capodimonte Palace.

ROYAL NAPLES

For many people, their first encounter with Naples is at the main passenger port, the **Stazione Marittima di Molo Beverello**. It is a good place to start, right in the centre, with the city laid out panoramically before you and the heartland of Aragonese and Bourbon royal Naples just across the road.

Walk up into the large workmanlike **Piazza Municipio** (Municipal Square), where the **Chiesa di San Giacomo degli Spagnoli** (St James of the Spanish) was built by the Viceroy in 1540 (rebuilt in 1741) as a tribute to the patron saint of Spain.

Castel Nuovo★★

To the left, the forbidding **Castel Nuovo★★** (New Castle; ☎ *081-795 2003*) (KZ), also known **Maschio Angioino** (Angevin Keep), was built by the Angevins in 1279 to replace

Sturdy round towers mark out the five corners of the imposing Castel Nuovo.

two earlier royal residences, the Castel dell'Ovo (*see* p.39) and the Castello di Capuana (now the city law courts). It was almost entirely reconstructed by the Aragonese king, Alfonso il Magnanimo in 1443. At the entrance the masterly **Arco di Trionfo di Alfonso**★★ (Triumphal Arch of Alfonso) was designed by Francesco Laurana in 1467. Inside, the **Sala dei Baroni** (Barons' Hall), with a magnificent rib vaulted ceiling, is now the city Council Chamber. The **Cappella Palatina** (Palatine Chapel), the only surviving part of the 13C castle, and three floors of the west wing house the **Museo Civico** (City Museum), with mainly 14C-19C paintings, sculptures and *objets d'art*, which together offer a fascinating history of the city. There are excellent views from the top floors.

Teatro San Carlo★

Up the hill, the rather bland exterior of the **Teatro San Carlo**★ (San Carlo Opera House; *Via San Carlo,* ☎ *081-797 2331. Guided tours*

Sitting transfixed in a gilded box at the Teatro San Carlo, one of the world's finest and most lavishly decorated opera houses, listening to voices soar to the rafters in an aria from Cosi Fan Tutte – inspirational!

Glass and iron elegance in the Galleria Umberto I.

The lively Piazza del Plebiscito, with Caffè Gambrinus on the right. In the background are ʼthe Castel Sant'Elmo (left) and Certosa di San Martino (right).

Sat-Sun 2-3.30pm) (KZ T⁴) belies the gilded opulence within. This is the oldest opera house in Italy, originally built in 1737, and rebuilt after a fire in 1816. It has 184 boxes, arranged in six tiers, and seats an audience of 3 000. Among its most notable artistic directors were Scarlatti, Bellini, Verdi and Donizetti (the premiere of *Lucia de*

Lammermoor was held here). It still ranks as one of the premier opera houses of the world (for booking details, *see* p.107).

Across the pretty **Piazza Trieste e Trento**, which sadly doubles as a turning circle for half the city's buses, the **Galleria Umberto I** (KZ) (1887) used to rank as one of the ritziest shopping malls in the world, with a patterned marble pavement, and towering elaborately decorative galleries, topped by a glass and iron dome as intricate and delicate as a spider's web.

Piazza del Plebiscito★

Cross the piazza (JKZ) and stop for coffee and a sticky cake at the **Caffè Gambrinus** (*see* p.101), one of the city's oldest and most glamorous cafés. Gather here at the

weekends for a fascinating and unusual tour of **Underground Naples** (*Associazione Culturale Napoli e la città sotterranea, Vico S. Anna di Palazzo 52, ☎ 081-400 256. Tours Sat 10am, 6pm; Sun and festivals 10am, 11am, 6pm; Fri 9pm*). As far back as the 5C BC, the Neapolitans realised that it was easy to carve the tufa rock on which the city rests, and over the centuries it has become honeycombed by tunnels, warehouses and cellars.

Walk on into the **Piazza del Plebiscito★**, originally laid out as a parade ground in 1810. At the far end is the imposing neo-Classical **Basilica di San Francesco di Paola** (JZ), built in 1817 by architect Pietro Bianchi as a celebration of King Ferdinand's restoration to the throne. It is a close copy of the Pantheon in Rome.

A curving colonnade frames the Basilica di San Francesco di Paola, at one end of the Piazza del Plebiscito.

Palazzo Reale★ (Royal Palace)
Opposite, a line of eight stone Neapolitan kings marks the entrance to the **Palazzo Reale★** (Royal Palace; ☎ *081-580 8111*)

Opposite the Basilica is the Palazzo Reale.

(KZ). This vast, dour, symmetrical palace could only be Spanish. The Viceroy initiated construction in 1600, nominally for a state visit by Philip III. The visit never took place, conveniently leaving his emissary in control of one of the grandest royal buildings in 17C Europe. The first king took possession only in 1743. Building continued intermittently until 1843.

The magnificent staircase of the Palazzo Reale.

A monumental double staircase leads up to the lavishly decorated and furnished

State Apartments★, of which 30 are open to the public, starting with a charming private theatre, the **Teatrino di Corte**, and ending with the splendidly ornate 19C **Cappella Reale** (Royal Chapel).

The **'Ala delle Feste'** wing is now home to the **Biblioteca Nazionale** (National Library), one of the most important historical libraries in Italy, with several medieval manuscripts and parchments recovered from Herculaneum. The **Stables** are used for temporary exhibitions.

The ornate Guglia dell'Immacolata (Spire of Mary Immaculata), on Piazza del Gesù Nuovo, is an important example of Neopolitan sculpture.

THE CENTRO STORICO (HISTORIC CITY CENTRE)

Begin the walk at Piazza Trieste e Trento (*see* p.23), and walk uphill along **Via Toledo**, one of the most famous shopping streets in Naples, named after the Viceroy who commissioned it in 1536. Just to the west, the mainly 16C **Quartieri Spagnoli** (Spanish Quarter) (JZ) has some fine but crumbling Baroque architecture, in one of the poorest and most densely populated districts of the inner city, with walls propped up by scaffolding and washing festooned across the streets. Visitors can be vulnerable to petty crime in this part of town, so be on the alert when walking around here. The **Sant'Anna dei Lombardi (Chiesa di Monteoliveti)** (*Piazza*

26

Monteoliveto 3) (KYZ) was built in 1411 by the Aragonese kings, who commissioned paintings and **sculptures★** from many leading 15C artists. The finest is an eight-figure group, *Compianto sul Cristo morto* (Mourning over a Dead Christ) by Guido Mazzoni (1492).

Piazza del Gesù Nuovo

Go right into **Piazza del Gesù Nuovo**, the heart of old Naples (KY). In the centre is the **Guglia dell'Immacolata** (Spire of Mary Immaculata), erected in 1743 by the Jesuits.

The **Chiesa del Gesù Nuovo** (New Church of Jesus) has an extraordinary studded stone façade, rather like cardboard packaging. Both this and the Renaissance entrance were originally intended to be the wall of the 15C Palazzo Sanseverino, but this palace was never finished. In 1584 the building was bought by the Jesuits who transformed it

The strange façade of the Chiesa del Gesù Nuovo belies the church's elaborate Baroque interior.

into the present opulent Baroque church, with every available surface decorated in multicoloured marble, gilding and frescoes. The 19C altar is inlaid with semi-precious stones.

Spaccanapoli★★

Via Benedetto Croce forms the first leg of what is commonly known as the **Spaccanapoli★★** (Split-Naples), an ancient Greek thoroughfare which still bisects the old city (KY). Straight ahead is the free-standing belfry of **Santa Chiara★**, built in 1310-28 by Sancia de Mallorca, wife of King Robert the Wise, as a Poor Clare convent. The church is remarkably plain for this otherwise lavishly embellished city, but was only restored to its original elegant simplicity after massive bomb damage in 1943. Near the altar is the magnificent **tomb★★** of Robert the Wise (d. 1343), by

Sit awhile in the cloisters of Santa Chiara – suddenly you're so far from the madding crowd.

Florentine sculptors Giovanni and Pacio Bertini.

The entrance to the **cloisters★** and **museum** is round the side of the church, along Via Santa Chiara (*admission to the museum*). In 1742, Domenico Antonio Vaccaro took the already beautiful Gothic cloisters and transformed them into an almost frivolous magic garden, with pillars and walls covered with splendid **majolica tiles★**, and shady vines covering the walkways. It is the perfect place for soothing the troubles of the careworn. The small museum has various church treasures and a display on the renovation.

Continue along Spaccanapoli, which develops into a charming street, ideal for window shopping, full of delis, bookshops, and boutiques. A couple of blocks further on, you come out into **Piazza San Domenico Maggiore** (KY 139). Although originally built in 1238, the exterior of the **Basilica di San Domenico Maggiore** was massively altered in 1506 and the interior again remodelled in 1850-53 in a neo-Gothic style. The Cappellone del Crocifisso is home to a miraculous crucifix, which supposedly spoke to St Thomas Aquinas, who lived nearby. There are also 45 Aragonese tombs and some 14C frescoes, thought to be by Pietro Cavallini, a pupil of Giotto.

The Guglia di San Domenico, on the Piazza San Domenico Maggiore, was built to give thanks for release from the 1656 plague.

Take the little alley to the right off the square, Via de Sanctis, to visit the enchanting little **Cappella Sansevero** (Sansevero Chapel; ☎ *081-551 8470*), built in the late 16C as a funeral chapel for the di Sangro family. The frescoes and other paintings are beautiful, but are far outshone by some extraordinary **sculptures★**, of which the finest is the haunting *Veiled Christ* by Giuseppe Sanmartino. On either side of the altar are *Chastity* (a veiled woman) and *Despair* (a man struggling with a net). In the crypt are two skeletons with 'petrified' veins, the property of a notorious 18C alchemist, Raimondo di Sangro.

Continue along Spaccanapoli to the 15C **Chiesa di Sant'Angelo a Nilo**, a highlight of which is the tomb of Cardinal Rinaldo Brancaccio, sculpted by Donatello in 1426. A little further on, **Piazzetta del Nilo** is home to one of the famous landmarks of Naples, the **Corpo di Napoli** (Body of Naples). This Roman statue of a reclining man, depicting the God of the Nile, went missing for centuries. When it was rediscovered, headless, people thought the cherubs representing the river's tributaries, were at their mother's breast, and claimed the statue represented the mother-city. It was the 17C before its head (male) was restored.

Just beyond this is the second leg of Spaccanapoli, **Via San Biagio dei Librai**, a treasure trove of antiques and handicrafts (KLY). Turn right onto Via Duomo if you want to visit the **Museo Civico Filangieri** (Filangieri Museum), a late 15C palace and 16C monastery. Largely rebuilt in the 19C, the **Palazzo Como★** now houses a fine art collection, based around the private collection of Prince Gaetano Filangieri.

The Corpo di Napoli (Body of Naples), depicting the God of the Nile.

Alternatively, turn left onto **Via San Gregorio Armeno**, a charming street lined by shops and workshops selling *presepi* (*see* pp.5, 106). The **Chiesa di San Gregorio Armeno** (Church of St Gregory of Armenia; *cloisters open daily 9.30am-noon, church open Tues 8am-1pm*) was founded in the 8C, by a group of nuns fleeing religious persecution in Byzantium, taking with them the relics of St Gregory. The lavishly decorated **interior★** has 18C frescoes by Luca Giordano, two Baroque **organs**, and a magnificent 16C gilded wood ceiling. In the cloister is a charming fountain (1733) depicting Christ and the Samaritan.

At the top of the street on the right, the **Chiesa di San Lorenzo Maggiore** (Church of St Lawrence; *Piazza San Gaetano,* ☎ *081-454 948*) was built in 1265. It was here that Boccaccio first met his muse, Fiammetta, and at the same time Petrarch was resident in the adjoining monastery. The current façade, portal and doors date to the 14C, while the **interior★** is one of the most

31

sumptuous of the many Baroque
extravagances in the city. From the cloister
of the adjoining monastery, you can visit
archaeological excavations which have
unearthed many incarnations of the city,
dating from the days of the Ancient Greeks
to the Middle Ages.

Decumanus Maximus★★

Turn right and you will find yourself on that
other great thoroughfare of Old Naples,
Via Tribunali★ (KLY). This follows the
course of the **Decumanus Maximus★★**, or
main east-west street of the ancient Greco-
Roman grid plan, running parallel with
Spaccanapoli. Along this vital backbone of
the city, there are many more churches for
those who haven't yet had their fill.

*The neo-Gothic
façade of the
Duomo di San
Gennaro belies its
early medieval
origins.*

A left turning into Via Duomo takes you to the **Duomo di San Gennaro** (Cathedral of St Jannarius). Built by the Angevins and consecrated in 1315, it has, like all churches in Naples, been considerably altered over the years, most recently with a late 19C Gothic façade. Inside, the central nave has a fine 17C gilded wood ceiling and frescoes by Luca Giordano. The **Cappella del Tesoro di San Gennaro** holds the city's most precious and famous relic, two phials of the blood of San Gennaro, patron saint of Naples. Twice a year, in May and September, this miraculously liquifies, taken as a sign of fortune for the city and heralded with great celebration. The occasional glitch is taken to be a portent of disaster.

Other points of interest include **archaeological excavations** of the Greco-Roman town, a 5C **Baptistery** and the early Christian **Basilica di Santa Restituta**, which was grafted onto the new cathedral as a side chapel.

Next door, in Piazza Riario Sforza, the **Guglia di San Gennaro** is a monumental spire, erected to thank the saint for saving the city from the eruption of 1631. Just beyond this, **Pio Monte della Misericordia**, founded as a charitable institution in 1601 to help the poor, the ill and Christian slaves freed from the Ottomans, has some magnificent paintings, including an altarpiece depicting **The Seven Works of Mercy★★★** by Caravaggio.

You can make a short detour from Via Tribunali at this point, walking a couple of blocks north of the cathedral (beyond the **Porta San Gennaro**, painted by Mattia Preti in 1656 as a votive offering for being spared from the plague), to take in the **Chiesa di**

San Giovanni a Carbonara★ (*open Mon-Sat 9am-1pm*). This was founded as an Augustin monastery in 1343, and enlarged in the early 15C by King Ladislas, who is buried here (d. 1414) in a vast, beautifully carved monumental tomb. The round Cappella Caracciolo del Sole (1427) has a Tuscan tiled floor, while the Cappella Caracciolo del Vico (1517) opposite contains several fine paintings. The façade has a grand double

The Porta San Gennaro has a bust of the saint on one side (shown here) and a fresco by Mattia Preti on the other.

Right: The composer Vincenzo Bellini oversees the attractive square named after him.

In the heart of the raucous city, turn a quiet page in the oasis of calm, while savouring a glass of Greco di Tufo.

staircase added by Ferdinando Sanfelice in the early 18C.

Return to the Duomo and turn back along the Via Tribunali. At the far end, **Piazza Bellini** is one of the liveliest and prettiest squares in the old town, a pedestrianised area planted up with trees and greenery and with plenty of cafés for a well-earned rest. Try the Caffè Letterario Intra Moenia, a café combined with a bookstore, where you can browse the books and take in the art exhibitions while enjoying a drink. Just off the square, the **Accademia di Belle Artie** (Academy of Fine Arts) is an 18C convent, converted to an art gallery in 1840 and still housing an important collection of 19C Neapolitan paintings.

From here, walk through the tunnelled **Porta d'Alba** (KY), one of the original city gates, now lined with bookshops, into the chaotic bustle of the elegant 18C **Piazza Dante**, where the atmosphere is currently troubled by the exhausts of a hundred buses and the perennial works on the new metro.

MUSEO ARCHEOLOGICO NAZIONALE★★★ (NATIONAL ARCHAEOLOGICAL MUSEUM)

The **Museo Archeologico Nazionale★★★** (*Piazza Museo 19,* ☎ *081-292 823. Open Wed-Mon 9am-2pm, though some departments close at 1.30pm*) (KY) is a world-class collection. The frustrating thing about it is not only the limited opening times, but the fact that at any given moment, half of the museum may be shut.

On the ground floor is a superb collection of **Greco-Roman sculpture★★★**, some found locally at Pompeii, Herculaneum, and others part of the Farnese Collection inherited by Charles III Bourbon from his mother, Elizabeth Farnese. The highlights are a magnificent statue of *Hercules*, the huge complex *Farnese Bull*, both from the Caracalla Baths in Rome, and a 2C AD statue of the many-breasted *Artemis* from Ephesus.

On the mezzanine floor to the left are the fabulous **Pompeii mosaics★★**, from the *Cave Canem* ('beware of the dog') sign to the remarkable mosaic from the House of the Faun, depicting *Alexander the Great* trouncing King Darius of Persia. To the right, the **Napoli Antica Gallery★★★** houses exhibits on the history of Naples, along with a series of votive terracotta **heads★**.

On the first floor, to the left, are a

collection of **small bronzes, silver, glass and ivory★★** from Pompeii and Herculaneum, followed by a partial reconstruction of the **Temple of Isis★★★**, Pompeii, displaying the many pictures and objects found there. The third section is the jewel, displaying in all their glory the fabulous **frescoes★★★** found at Pompeii, Herculaneum and Stabia. The right, on the first floor, is dedicated to finds from the **Villa di Pisone★★★** (or Villa dei Papiri), in Herculaneum, which was itself a museum. These include a library of 800

The entrance to the Museo Archeologico Nazionale, one of the world's most important archaeological collections.

parchments (photos only on display). Behind this are the **gems**, of which the greatest piece is the cameo *Farnese Cup*. A detailed paper, cork and wood **model of Pompeii** (1861-79) and a fine **Egyptian collection** on the lower ground floor make up the rest of the highlights of a stupendous museum.

CHIAIA AND THE LUNGOMARE

Santa Lucia★★

The city's seafront is neatly divided into two almost equal sections by the traditional fishermen's quarter of **Santa Lucia★★**. Little now remains of the area's tightly packed slum dwellings. The expansion westwards of 'royal Naples' began in the early 18C and development has continued ever since.

Most of the Santa Lucia seafront is now

The picturesque Borgo Marinaro quarter is full of trendy cafés and trattoria.

lined by some of the city's largest and most glamorous hotels, while the off-shore **Borgo Marinaro**, the harbour and village at the foot of the castle, has become a marina, one of the city's trendiest restaurant quarters, and a wonderful place to sit under the stars on a warm summer's evening. To the east are the working dockyards, to the west, the sweeping seafront known simply as the **Lungomare**, whose relaxing atmosphere is tempered slightly by the busy through road just behind it.

The **Castel dell'Ovo** (Castle of the Egg), the city's greatest landmark and oldest castle, gets its curious name from a 14C legend that the poet Virgil, who had something of a reputation as a magician, placed a magic egg in the castle's foundations. As long as the egg remained intact, no great harm would come to the city.

The tufa walls of the Castel dell'Ovo rise up from the sea.

The castle was actually built by the Angevins in 1128, since when it has been blown up at least twice and almost entirely rebuilt several times. The most recent restoration transformed it into one of the world's most glamorous conference centres. From the jetty there are splendid **views★★** of Vesuvius to the east and the Bay of Naples to the west.

On shore, the magnificent **Fontana dell'Immacolatella** (Immacolata Fountain) was sculpted in 1601 by Michelangelo Naccherino and Pietro Bernini.

Villa Comunale
Beyond Santa Lucia is a long, thin, rather scruffy public park known as the **Villa Comunale**, first laid out in 1697 and flanked

The Villa Pignatelli was modelled on a Pompeiian design.

The attractive small harbour at Mergellina is always bustling with activity.

by two grand piazzas, Piazza Vittoria and Piazza della Republicca. In it is the city's aquarium, the **Acquario** (☎ *081-583 3263*), which opened in 1872 making it the oldest in Europe. The fish displayed are all found in the Naples area. About halfway along, the **Museo Principe di Aragona Pignatelli Cortes** (*Riviera di Chiaia,* ☎ *081-669 675. Open Tues-Sun 9am-2pm*) is a neo-Classical villa built in 1826 by Pietro Valente. It is named after its last owner, Prince Diego Aragona Pignatelli Cortes, whose granddaughter donated it to the state. Along with the sumptuously furnished rooms, there are many fine 18C-19C paintings, sculptures and ceramics, and a small collection of carriages.

Mergellina★

From here it is possible to continue around the bay to **Mergellina★**, where a row of cafés lines the shore, offering spectacular **views★★**

of the city and bay and excellent ice-cream. On the hill above is supposedly the **Tomba di Virgilio** (*Parco Virgiliano, Via Salita Grotta*), the tomb of the Roman poet, Virgil. The Roman tomb actually has nothing to do with him, but the park does contain the tomb of the poet, Giacomo Leopardi, whose remains were brought here from his birthplace, Recanati, in the Marches.

Looking up Via F. Acton, towards the Certosa di San Martino.

Take a bus to the outer suburb of **Posillipo★**, where some superb 17C-19C villas have gradually been overwhelmed by high-rise development. The best way to see them is by sea, en route to Procida, but there are superb **views** of Naples from the cape.

Chiaia

Walk up one of the many narrow streets leading inland from the Riviera di Chiaia and almost immediately you begin to climb steeply into the district of **Chiaia**, the ritziest shopping area of Naples, with small, very smart streets full of designer boutiques, leading between the key points of **Piazza Amedeo**, **Piazza dei Martiri** and on to Piazza del Plebiscito (*see* p.24).

VOMERO

Another largely 19C residential district, reached by three funicular railways, Vomero crowns the peak behind the city.

Sant'Elmo and San Martino★★

The star-shaped **Castel Sant'Elmo** (*Via Tito Angeline*) was built in 1537-46 by Viceroy Toledo to replace a crumbling Angevin fortress at the outer defensive wall of the city. It proved to be of more use to various governors and monarchs hiding from rebellions, and also spent several centuries as a prison. There is little to see inside, but it does afford good views.

At its feet, with the same stunning **views**, sits the **Certosa di San Martino★★** (JZ)

(Monastery of St Martin; *Largo San Martino 5*, ☎ *081-578 1769. Open Tues-Sun 9am-2pm*), constructed by the Duke of Calabria in 1325 as a Carthusian monastery. It has been a **museum★** since 1866.

The Carthusian order was never short of money, and the monks of San Martino used it to good advantage. From the 15C-19C they built up an incomparable collection of paintings, sculpture, ceramics, glass, jewellery, **presepi★★** and other Neapolitan figurines. The Prior, whose rooms, the **Quarto del Priore**, have been carefully reconstructed, lived like a potentate,

surrounded by these treasures. In 1623-56, architect and sculptor, Cosimo Fanzago, took charge of the total redecoration of the church **interior★★**, creating a symphony of Baroque extravagance, with multicoloured marble festooned with garlands of fruit and flowers and studded with *putti* (cherubs), surrounding frescoes by Luca Giordano and paintings by Caracciolo, Guido Reni and Simon Vouet. The complex also has two early 17C cloisters. As in the Archaeological Museum, large sections may be closed at any given moment.

The Quarto del Priore (Prior's Residence) in the Certosa di San Martino offers fine views of the bay.

Villa Floridiana★

Further along the ridge, the 18C neo-Classical **Villa Floridiana★** (rebuilt in 1817) is home to the **Museo Nazionale di Ceramica Duca di Martina★** (Duke of Martina National Ceramic Museum; ☎ 081-578 8418. Open Tues-Sun 9am-2pm), whose grandiose name rather outstrips its station. Nevertheless, it is an attractive museum with interesting collections of ceramics, majolica, glass, leather, Gothic ivory, enamels and 18C Neapolitan sketches. From the gardens there is a splendid **panorama★**.

CAPODIMONTE

The area north of the Archaeological Museum and old city walls was used by everyone, as far back as the Greeks, as a cemetery. As a result, along with the inevitable clutch of churches are some fascinating, sometimes gruesome cemeteries and catacombs, of which the finest are undoubtedly the **Catacombe di San Gennaro★★** (*Via Capodimonte 13*, ☎ 081-741 1071. Tours daily 9.30, 10.15, 11 and

11.45am), further up the hill. This huge two-storey web of galleries, opening into a baptistery and basilica, was all hewn from the soft volcanic rock. First used in the 2C AD, it acquired its first Christian saint, Sant'Agrippina, in the 3C. San Gennaro (of the miraculous blood) was buried here in the 6C, and suddenly people were fighting for space. All bishops of Naples were buried here until the 11C and there are some fine 2C-10C frescoes and mosaics.

The former royal palace of Capodimonte has always been home to great works of art, for Charles III originally built it partly to house his collection.

Palazzo e Galleria Nazionale de Capodimonte★★
(Capodimonte Palace and Art Gallery)

At the top of the hill is the last of the great royal palaces, built by Charles III from 1738 onwards, partly as residence, partly to house the huge Farnese collection he had recently inherited. It was only completed a century later. In 1742, Ferdinando Sanfelice was commissioned to lay out the **park★**, and in 1743 Ferdinando Fuga was put in charge of constructing a royal porcelain works in the grounds. Its output, specialising in delicate figurines and flowers, became famous throughout Europe. The royal pleasure palace also had a pheasantry, hunting lodge, zoo (complete with elephants and lions), and a greenhouse, to grow pineapples and other exotic fruit.

Today, the vast palace has become the **Palazzo e Galleria Nazionale di Capodimonte★★** (*Capodimonte Palace and Art Gallery;* ☎ *081-749 9111. Open Tues-Sat 10am-7pm, Sun 9am-2pm*), home to the finest collection of paintings in Italy. Highlights of the **Pinacoteca★★**, which has recently been reorganised and extended, include works by Raphael, Botticelli, Lippi, Caravaggio, El Greco, Bruegel and Goya. There are also suites of ostentatiously furnished royal **apartments**, culminating in the glorious **Salottino di porcellana★** (Porcelain Room), which is completely lined with about 3 000 tiles of Capodimonte porcelain. Other sections of this huge museum contain a fine collection of **majolica and porcelain** including Capodimonte ware, and a 19C biscuitware group showing the Procession of Aurora, the **royal armoury**, ivories, watches and other *objets d'art*.

MUST SEE

Pompeii★★★
Although a prosperous Roman trading city, **Pompeii★★★** would probably have faded into obscurity were it not for its abrupt and violent death, buried under a massive volcanic eruption in AD 79. Frozen in time and superbly preserved, excavations have been going on for nearly 250 years, making this the single most important Roman archaeological site in the world.

Vesuvio★★★ (Vesuvius)
Towering over the Bay of Naples, **Mt Vesuvius★★★** is the last major volcano still active on the European mainland. The walk to the crater provides tourists with high drama and fantastic **views★★★**. Its uncertain temper remains a constant source of worry to the nearly 2 million people threatened by its next eruption.

Ercolano★★ (Herculaneum)
A trendy Roman coastal resort, **Herculaneum★★** was also engulfed by the eruption of AD 79. The excavated area is tiny in comparison to Pompeii, but the seamless continuity of modern Ercolano above makes the ruins come effortlessly to life.

Capri★★★
Emperor Tiberius loved this island so much that he moved the whole Roman court here. Artists and intellectuals, from Alexandre Dumas to Graham Greene, have also been drawn by its magnificent scenery. Today, along with the **Blue Grotto★★**, this distinctly upmarket destination offers designer shopping in a perfectly designed setting.

Sorrento★★

Since the Grand Tour of the 18C, tourists have flocked to this charming little town. It is a perfect base from which to explore the whole region, with excellent transport, fabulous views across the bay, good restaurants and souvenir shops and a choice of 120 hotels.

Attractive Positano enjoys a spectacular setting.

The Amalfi Coast★★★

A winding road hugs the cliff face of the **Costiera Amalfitana★★★**, one of the Mediterranean's most spectacularly beautiful stretches of scenery, joining the pretty resort town of **Positano★★★** to historic **Amalfi★★**, with its superbly decorated cathedral, and the charming mountain village of **Ravello★★★**.

WEST OF NAPLES –
THE CAMPI FLEGREI★★

This beautiful cape to the west of Naples has been popular among wealthy Neapolitans and fishermen alike since the ancient Greeks first settled the area in the 8C BC. Its increasingly dense population, with Naples effectively sprawling out to link its towns into one giant conurbation, is all the more extraordinary because the area is known as the **Campi Flegrei★★** (Phlegraean 'burning' Fields). Forty small volcanoes smoulder beneath the surface, and even out to sea, creating hundreds of hot springs and fumaroles. Astonishingly, far from deterring development, it is this volcanic activity that has proved to be one of the area's greatest attractions – the Romans were quick to build baths, temples and sybaritic playgrounds wherever they found hot springs. The ancients believed that volcanic **Lago d'Averno★** (Lake Avernus), to the west of Pozzuoli, was the entrance to Hades, while Dante is said to have drawn much of his inspiration for the *Inferno* from these grumbling lands.

Pozzuoli★
Bus from the Lungomare in Naples to the entrance of the Solfatara. Alternatively, take the Cumana train, which involves a steep walk (Giranapoli tickets accepted on both).
First settled by Greeks in 530 BC, under the Romans **Pozzuoli★** became an important trading and industrial centre, whose fortunes slowly faded as its harbour was drowned.

Today, the star attraction is undoubtedly the **Solfatara★★** (*Via Solfatara 161, ☎ 081-526 2341*), a huge shallow volcanic crater

Exploring the I C AD underground chambers of the amphitheatre, Pozzuoli.

originally formed about 4 000 years ago. It last erupted in 1198, but it is still the most visibly active volcano in the region, with a dramatic collection of steaming vents, bubbling jets of sand, boiling pools of mud and mustard-yellow heaps of sulphurous rock.

Downhill, towards the town centre, the imposingly complete **Anfiteatro Flavio★★** (amphitheatre; *Via Terracciano*, ☎ *081-526 6007*), built in AD 69-79 and seating 40 000 people, has well-preserved **basements★★** and equipment used to hoist caged animals into the arena. The picturesque **Rione Terra** (old town) had to be evacuated in 1970 because of the dramatic upward movement of the ground; restoration has only just begun and most of the area is currently inaccessible.

Terme di Baia★★

Further along the coast, Baia thrived as a Roman spa. The highlight now is the **Castello Aragonese**, virtually rebuilt by the

51

Spanish viceroy, Don Pedro de Toledo, in 1538, which is now home to the **Museo Archeologico dei Campi Flegrei** (Phlegraean Fields Archaeology Museum; ☎ *081-523 3797. Open Mon-Fri 9am-1hr before sunset*). The town also has an imposingly large complex of **Terme Romane** (Roman Baths, *Via Fusaro 35;* ☎ *081-868 7592. Open daily 9am-1hr before sunset*). At nearby **Bacoli**, the **Piscina Mirabile★** (*Via A. Greco. Open daily 9am-1hr before sunset*) is a vast underground reservoir carved from the tufa by the Romans to supply the fleet, based at Miseno.

SOUTH OF NAPLES

Vesuvio★★★ (Vesuvius)

Take a bus (Giranapoli tickets accepted) or Circumvesuviana train to Ercolano. Infrequent tourist buses climb the mountain, leaving from outside the railway station (ask the nearby tourist office for details). From outside the station, for relatively little more cost, it is possible to take a shared minibus taxi which will give you about 2hrs at the summit. Allow 30-45 mins for the winding 600m (650yd) walk from the car park to the summit (1 281m/4 163ft). The path is good but steep, and there is no shade. Wear a hat and shoes with a good grip, take water and avoid the midday heat.

Driving up the hairpin bends, the weathered walls of a much larger, earlier crater become obvious. The smooth, rusty brown cone of the upper reaches of Vesuvius is only the offspring of a giant volcano, **Monte Somma**, thought originally to have been three times the height.

Once at the top, the path takes a flatter, but precipitous course along the ridge between the vast central crater, a plunging

Mount Vesuvius, bathed in the warm evening sunshine.

red and grey rocky bowl 200m (655ft) deep and 600m (1 970ft) in diameter, and the spectacular **view★★★** across the whole Bay of Naples.

Vesuvius is a relative youngster in volcanic terms, first blowing its stack about 12 000 years ago. Since the disastrous eruption of AD 79 there have been over 100 more, although only those in 1631, 1794 and its last spectacular, in 1944, have caused severe damage.

A few tiny puffs of smoke are all that is now visible within the crater, but these belie the forces building up inside the magma chamber, 8km (5 miles) below the surface.

Vesuvius will erupt again and because its main fissure has been plugged by rock, geologists are agreed that this time the eruption will be explosive. With the city encroaching ever further onto its slopes, and around 2 million people living in the vicinity, it is a race against time to implement proper plans for evacuation.

Pompeii★★★
Take the Circumvesuviana train to Pompeii Villa dei Misteri station, about 200m (220yds) from the main Porta Marina entrance, or to Pompeii Scavi station which is in the actual town of Pompeii and enables you to enter the ruins through the Porta del Anfiteatro. This second

Ever-present, Vesuvius watches and waits over the Forum, Pompeii.

option may be preferable, as all the tourist buses stop at the Villa dei Misteri which can get very crowded, but does involve a longer walk. Open daily 9am-1hr before dusk. Admission. June-Sept, evening son et lumière performances (☎ 081-857 5111 for details).

Imagine any prosperous modern town, with its shops and houses, restaurants and bars, marketplace and churches, populated by rich and poor. Imagine you are free to wander into every house, poking through the lives of people who seem to have just stepped out for a moment. It takes a long time and a lot of walking to see Pompeii properly. Most of the tours choose one of three set routes, cherry-picking plum sites and whistling through in two hours. It is cheaper and far more exciting to buy a detailed site guidebook and map, or hire a speaker wand, equip yourself with a hat, comfortable shoes and water, and spend the whole day exploring. There is a cafeteria (with shop and toilets) near the Forum, where you can enjoy a drink or snack.

Bronze statue of the Dancing Faun, from the Casa del Fauno.

A Thriving Port

By the time of the eruption, Pompeii was almost 1000 years old. Only in 80 BC was it conquered by Rome and renamed Colonia Veneria Cornelia Pompeii, after its conqueror, Pompey.

The city was laid out on classical lines, with a 3km- (2 mile) long wall and eight city gates, within which a grid of narrow paved streets radiated out from the central forum. Lead pipes carried water

under the pavements to the public
fountains, baths, and the homes of the
wealthy. Its population of about 10 000
(some 60 per cent free men, the rest slaves)
flourished through trade, for Pompeii was
only 500m (540yds) from the sea until the
eruption pushed the coastline back a
staggering 2km (1.5 miles).

Map of Pompeii

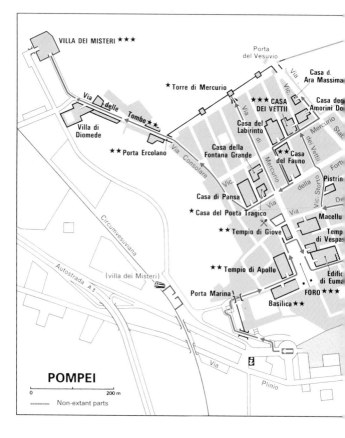

250 Years of Excavations

After the eruption, the city was totally forgotten until the late 16C, and it was 1748 before Bourbon King Charles III ordered proper excavations, which have been going on ever since. In 1860, Giuseppi Fiorelli poured liquid plaster into a hole, reconstructing, to his amazement, the

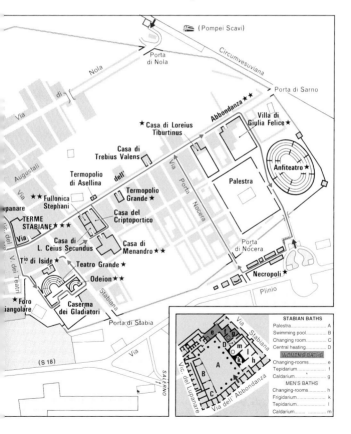

STABIAN BATHS

Palestra	A
Swimming pool	B
Changing room	C
Central heating	D

WOMEN'S BATHS

Changing-rooms	e
Tepidarium	f
Caldarium	g

MEN'S BATHS

Changing-rooms	h
Frigidarium	k
Tepidarium	l
Caldarium	m

agonised figure of a Pompeiian citizen. Around 80 per cent of the town has now been uncovered, and the remarkably preserved houses, frescoes and mosaics are being carefully restored.

The most fragile finds – from the bodies to the finest frescoes and mosaics, jewellery and furniture, the bread found in a baker's oven or the plate of pasta and beans near the brothel door – have been removed for safety to the Archaeological Museum in Naples. Nevertheless, the streets of Pompeii provide unparalleled insights into the ancient world.

Not to be Missed

The road from the entrance leads straight to the **Foro★★★** (Forum), the central market square, surrounded by the **Edifici Municipali** (Municipal Offices), **Comitium** (Assembly Room) and **Tempio di Apollo★★** (Temple of Apollo). Beyond the temple, the Via del Foro leads to the **Terme del Foro** (Forum Baths) and a residential area with several of the city's finest patrician villas, including the **Casa del Fauno★★** (House of the Faun), the **Casa della Fontana Grande** (House of the Large Fountain; *see* p.61), the **Casa degli Amorini Dorati★** (House of the Golden Cupids; closed to the public), and the magnificently decorated **Casa dei Vettii★★★** (House of the Vettii). Lined with tombs, the long side track called the **Via delle Tombe★★** leads out of the city, comprising the largest and most imposing of the city's cemeteries, to the lavishly wealthy **Villa dei Misteri★★★** (House of Mysteries) which stands outside the city walls.

Return to the forum, stopping en route at the **Lupanare** (Brothel) with its bawdy decorations, then head down the main street,

Strolling along the Via dell'Abbondanza, Pompeii, looking at the Roman fast food stalls, just waiting for a pot of pasta and reminding yourself that it is nearly 2 000 years since they last served a meal.

Via dell'Abbondanza★★. A couple of blocks on, at the crossroads with **Via Stabiana**, are the **Terme Stabiane★★★** (Stabian Baths). From here, Via Stabiana leads down to the entertainment area, where the **Teatro Grande★** (Large Theatre) is still in use for summer performances. Next to it are the **Odeon★★**, a covered, small theatre, originally used for concerts, and the **Caserma dei Gladiatori** (Arcaded Court of the Gladiators). Behind the Teatro Grande is the **Tempio d'Iside★**, the original decor of which is in Naples' Museo Archeologico. The extraordinarily complete Via dell'Abbondanza heads east past several more highly decorated villas to the **Anfiteatro★** (amphitheatre) and **Palestra Grande** (sports field), from where a road doubles back around the ongoing excavations to the **Orto dei Fuggiaschi** (Garden of the Fugitives), in which 27 bodies lie where they were discovered.

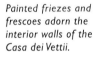

Painted friezes and frescoes adorn the interior walls of the Casa dei Vettii.

The Last Days of Pompeii

In AD 62, the Bay of Naples was shaken by a powerful earthquake. Over the next 17 years, there were increasingly frequent tremors, forcing local citizens to mend their cracked walls and frescoes with lime.

At noon on the 24 August, AD 79, a massive explosion literally blew the top off Mt Vesuvius. A mushroom cloud shot over 30km (18.5 miles) into the air, the sky grew black and a west wind brought a choking rain of ash and pumice down on Pompeii.

Across the bay, in Sorrento, a 17-year-old boy, Gaius Plinius Secundus (Pliny the Younger), wrote a terrifyingly vivid account of the disaster in two letters to the historian, Tacitus. His uncle, the admiral and naturalist, Pliny the Elder, took the fleet into the storm to attempt a rescue but died of a heart attack at Stabiae (now Castellamare).

So far, the wind direction

had spared Herculaneum from the falling ash, and many of those in Pompeii also survived this first onslaught, crawling over the pumice to survey the tattered remains of their once fine city.

Next day brought a new and even more terrible disaster. As the eruption slowed and the wind died down, the mushroom cloud collapsed. The debris of the shattered mountain turned into a tidal wave of super-heated rock, ash and dust known to vulcanologists as a pyroclastic flow. Travelling at a stunning 160kph (100mph), with searing temperatures of over 475°C (887°F), it engulfed both Herculaneum and Pompeii in minutes, the terrified citizens having time only to fling their hands up to their faces as they were engulfed in boiling stone.

No one knows why the people did not flee while they had the chance – some did run and survived. Yet over 5 000 bodies have been discovered in Pompeii, while at Herculaneum several hundred people have now been unearthed, huddled for shelter in a harbourside warehouse.

Left: Caserma dei Gladiatori (Arcaded Court of the Gladiators).
Above: The fountain in the Casa della Fontana Grande.

Ercolano** (Herculaneum)

Take a bus (Giranapoli tickets accepted) or Circumvesuviana train to Ercolano. Buses stop beside the gates of the excavation; from the train station, it is a walk of about 300m (320yds) downhill. Theatre performances are held in the ruins in summer. Open daily 9am-2hrs before dusk ☎ 081-739 0963.

Although an ancient city by the time the Romans arrived in about 290 BC, Herculaneum never achieved the same degree of wealth and status as Pompeii and remained a small, select resort where patrician families kept elegant seaside holiday villas.

The present site is far smaller than Pompeii, and relatively little more can be uncovered as the modern town of Ercolano was built over the ruins. In many ways,

The well-preserved Roman city of Ercolano (Herculaneum), most of which lies hidden below the modern town.

however, it is even more atmospheric, with modern houses remarkably similar in style to the ancient ones continuing seamlessly beyond the walls of the excavations, only differentiated by the lines of washing hanging from the modern windows. It is relatively easy to explore the whole site properly in a couple of hours, but for those in a hurry, highlights include the **Terme★★★** (Baths); the **Casa a Graticcio★★** (Trellis House), a double-storey wooden-framed apartment block; the **Casa del Mosaico di Nettuno e Anfitrite★★** (House of the Neptune and Amphitrite Mosaic), which has a stunning mosaic in its summer dining room; the **Casa dell' Atrio o Mosaico★★** (House of the Mosaic Atrium), with its geometric patterned mosaic floor; and the **Casa dei Cervi★★** (House of the Stags),

A number of the houses have remarkably well-preserved wall paintings.

a wealthy villa which was home to two magnificent statues of stags, now in the Naples museum. The **theatre** is just outside the main site, to the left of the entrance, on the road to Naples.

The Golden Mile

Follow the road from Herculaneum to the little town of **Portici**, along what is known as the **Miglio d'Oro** (Golden Mile). During the early 18C, the Bourbon kings built a palace, the **Reggia**, in Portici. Inevitably, the nobles followed suit and the area is stuffed with magnificent villas, most now in a terminal state of decay. The Reggia itself, which houses the Naples Department of Agriculture, has recently been restored and is open for occasional exhibitions or by appointment (*Via Università 100, Portici;* ☎ *081-775 1251*). The **Villa Campolieto** (*Corso Resina 283, Ercolano*) has also been restored and is open to the public.

Further south, in modern **Torre Annunziata**, built over the ruins of ancient **Oplontis**, another town wiped out by the AD 79 eruption, are the remains of the spectacular **Villa di Oplontis★★** (or Villa Poppaea), built by Emperor Nero's second wife, Poppaea, and decorated with magnificent **frescoes**.

THE ISLANDS

Capri★★★

*There are frequent hydrofoil services from Naples (Beverello and Mergellina), Sorrento and Ischia. From Capri's Marina Grande (ferry port), regular **boat trips** go to the Blue Grotto or tour right round the island. A cheap roundtrip ticket (Bigliette Cumulatavi) includes the funicular*

The Faraglioni Rocks punctuate Capri's eastern coastline.

from the harbour to Capri, and buses to Anacapri and the Blue Grotto. Within the towns, walking is obligatory; most of the roads are too narrow and steep for motorised transport.

Long since regarded as one of the most idyllic holiday destinations in the Mediterranean, the little island of Capri (6km/4 miles long by up to 3km/2 miles wide) really does have it all. Once attached

to the end of the Sorrentine Peninsula, its craggy rocks, limestone caves, tiny sandy coves and sapphire sea, make it an enchanting resort for sun and sea lovers. Add to this its charming little towns filled with gourmet restaurants, sun-drenched cafés and elegantly draped designer boutiques. Top it all off with country walks through spectacular scenery, just enough sightseeing to satisfy the restless, and cloak it in the scent of lemons, wild flowers and herbs. Little wonder then that Capri, the Island of Dreams, has captivated visitors from the Roman Emperors through to the 20C celebrities who have made their homes there.

Colourful fishing boats and seafood restaurants line the Marina Grande shoreline.

Capri Town★★★
This pretty little town straddles the neck of the island, between the massifs of Monte

Tiberio and Monte Solaro. On the eastern side, the **Marina Grande★** waterfront is home to the main port and several good seafood restaurants. In the 16C, with pirates raiding the coasts, most of the island's inhabitants moved uphill for safety, giving birth to Capri town. At its heart is the charming **Piazza Umberto I★**, known to locals simply as the **Piazzetta**, crammed with café tables and a hive of leisure activity around the clock.

From here, the narrow, flower-bedecked

The bustling 'Piazzetta' forms the heart of Capri town.

The Baroque dome of the church of Santo Stefano overlooks the Piazzetta.

alleys of the Arabesque medieval quarter stretch across the island to the **Certosa di San Giacomo** (Charterhouse of St James; *open Tues-Sun 9am-2pm*), a 14C Carthusian monastery whose simple white church and cloister now house a small collection of 17C-19C paintings, including some stormy canvases by German painter, Karl Wilhelm Diefenbach.

Nearby, the **Belvedere Cannone**★★ offers

Map of Capri

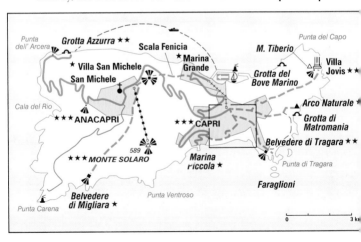

fabulous views along the cliff, over the pleasantly shady **Parco Augusto** (Gardens of Augustus), and down the hair-raising **Via Krupp★**, built by the German industrialist in 1902. Walk down this narrow, switchback road to the **Marina Piccola★**, once a tiny fishing village but now home to much of the island's beach tourism and water sports.

There are several other good walks in the area, but the best ones go to a giant arch of rock, the **Arco Naturale★**, and to the imposing **Villa Jovis★★** (Jupiter's Villa), 35-45 minutes' walk from town, one of 12 villas built on Capri by Emperor Tiberius, who moved the entire court here, ruling his far flung empire from the Villa Jovis for the last ten years of his life (AD 27-37).

Above: The vertiginous Via Krupp. Below: The Arco Naturale.

Anacapri★★★

Anacapri★★★ is a less elegant but nonetheless entertaining little town, with a detailed scale model of the island in the main square. A few minutes' walk away is the coolly elegant **Villa San Michele★**. Built by a Swedish doctor and writer, Axel Munthe, it uses many of the Roman remains found in the grounds as a surprising counterpoint to the understated Scandinavian design. Outside, lush shady gardens lead to a terrace with a spectacular **panorama★★★** of Capri, Marina Grande, Mt Tiberius and the

Wandering through the magical gardens at the Villa San Michele, with cool green shade and the scent of flowers, leading to a perfectly positioned gazebo high on the clifftop, with views of the whole island and sparkling sea.

Villa San Michele perches dizzily on the clifftop.

Maritime traffic jam in the Blue Grotto.

Faraglioni. The nearby **San Michele church** is worth a visit for its **majolica pavement★** depicting the Garden of Eden. A narrow spiral staircase leads to an upper level (where the organ stands) which gives a better view of the pavement.

From the Piazza Vittoria, a chairlift whisks you painlessly up to the summit of **Monte Solaro★★★**, the highest point on the island (589m/1 930ft), with superb **views★★★** across the entire island and the Bay of Naples.

On the coast below, a small fleet of rowing boats ferries hundreds of tourists from Marina Grande through a narrow opening in the cliff for a five-minute glimpse of the island's most famous landmark, the **Grotta Azzurra★★** (Blue Grotto). The colour inside is the most extraordinary clear, luminous blue, a trick of the light refracting off the white sand below the surface. It is possible to swim into the cave but it is probably best to do so once most of the boats have gone home.

Ischia★★★

There are regular hydrofoil and ferry services from Naples (Beverello and Mergellina), Pozzuoli, Sorrento and Capri. Every half hour, buses circle the island in both directions.

The largest of the three islands (10km/6 miles by 7km/4 miles), **Ischia★★★** lies opposite Capri, a continuation of the Campi Flegrei (*see* p.50). Its scenery is varied and attractive. The central volcanic mountains are sprinkled with thermal springs and the coast is fringed by fine sandy beaches. Popular amongst tourists in Roman times, it is now a relatively cheap mass market destination; locals simply refer to it as the 'German island'.

The ferry docks in the main town of **Ischia Porto★**, a popular resort town with good beaches and radioactive hot springs, said to

Map of Ischia

Ptª Cornacchia — Baia di S. Montano
Ptª di M. Vico
Casamicciola Terme
Lacco Ameno
S 270
Ischia Porto
0   2 km
266 △ M. Rotaro
Ptª d. Soccorso — **Forio**   Monterone
★ **ISCHIA**
Ischia Ponte
M. EPOMEO ★★★ 788
△ 502 M. Trippodi
★★ **Castello d'Ischia**
★ **Spiaggia di Citara**
Fontana
S 270
Piedimonte
Ptª Imperatore
Panza
Serrara Fontana
Barano d'Ischia
Marina dei Maronti
Capo Negro
Sant' Angelo ★
Capo Grosso
Ptª S. Pancrazio
Ptª S. Angelo

Ferries unload at the island's main town, Ischia Porto.

A tiny fishing port with bright coloured boats ready to set sail, cool waterfront cafés – summertime, and the living is easy!

have curative powers. Its older sister, **Ischia Ponte★**, clusters round the foot of the imposing **Castello d'Ischia★★** , crowning an off-shore islet reached via a short causeway. Its outer defensive walls contain a jumble of intensely picturesque but half-ruinous buildings. A lift takes you to the top, so you can explore the Aragonese castle ruins (*open Mar-mid Nov daily 9.30am-6.30/7pm*) and several churches tucked away in the narrow, tree- and flower-lined pathways. Set in the top of the castle, **Il Terrazzo** restaurant provides outstanding views over the bay.

The prettiest town on the island is **Sant'Angelo★**, built along a narrow isthmus and tiny islet on the steep southern shore. In the vicinity are hot springs at the **Terme Cavascura**, and a natural steam vent, the **Fumarole**. From nearby **Fontana**, a steep 50-minute walk takes you up to the top of the island's highest mountain, **Monte**

73

Epomeo★★★ (788m/2 561ft) for spectacular **panoramas** over the island and the Bay of Naples. Mules are available for the less energetic. For those who do not make it up the mountain, the belvedere near **Serrara Fontana** has equally breathtaking **views★★**, with the land below dropping sharply down to Sant'Angelo.

An Angevin cathedral, several churches and a monastery comprise the fortified Castello d'Ischia.

Elsewhere, the main resort towns of **Casamicciola Terme** and **Forio** have thermal springs, beaches, large hotels and brash pizzerias. Forio also has the remains of its no-nonsense city walls and several attractive small churches, while nearby **Lacco Ameno** has an archaeological museum in the 18C **Villa Arbusto**.

Procida★

Few tourists set foot on **Procida★**, the smallest and least developed of the three islands, also part of the Campi Flegrei. It is a charming place to wander around, past

The mushroom-shaped Fungo di Lacco Ameno is a prominent landmark of the resort of Lacco Ameno, Ischia.

sleepy pastel-painted fishing villages, through citrus and olive groves and past crumbling villas, to swim off relatively empty beaches and eat leisurely meals in the local trattoria. It is small enough (4km/2.5 miles long) to explore thoroughly in a day. Ferries dock at the main town of **Marina di Sancio Cattolico**, usually simply known as the **Marina Grande**, with a web of narrow alleys leading steeply uphill to the 16C **Castello** (castle), most recently used as a prison, and **Terra Murata** (walled town). Also up here is the **Certosa di San Michele Arcangelo** (Monastery of the Archangel Michael), with a lively painting by Giordano depicting Michael defending Procida from the Turks. Linked by a bridge, the crescent moon-shaped **Isolotto di Vivara** (Islet of Vivara) is a nature-reserve (*advance permission needed to visit*).

The best beaches are at **Chiaiolella**, at the far end of the island.

PENISOLA SORRENTINA★★
(THE SORRENTINE PENINSULA)

The Circumvesuviana train links all the major towns along the peninsula; alternatively, take a hydrofoil or ferry from Naples (Beverello and Mergellina), Capri or Ischia to Sorrento. There are also direct bus services from the airport and local orange buses linking the towns and outlying villages.

Sorrento and the Bay of Naples at night.

Unlike its northern counterpart, the southern arm of the Bay of Naples is not volcanic. It is a stunningly beautiful area, rich with sweet-smelling groves of oranges, lemons and olives. Even the scrubby wild vegetation is ablaze with flowers in spring and bathed in the scent of wild rosemary and thyme. Pale limestone cliffs tumble to cobalt seas, and in the hazy distance Vesuvius seems to float weightlessly above the horizon.

Castellammare di Stabia★

The peninsula officially begins at **Castellammare di Stabia★**, home of Italy's main naval base and a popular thermal resort, with 28 springs and thermal baths, the **Antiche Terme**, offering curative treatments. The town museum, the **Antiquarium★** (*currently being restored,* ☎ 081-871 4541 *for details*) displays some fine frescoes and stucco bas reliefs rescued from local Roman villas, of which the finest is the **Villa di Arianna**, which can be visited and which offers fine views of the Bay and Vesuvius.

From the station, a cablecar leads to the top of **Monte Faito★★** (*1 100m/3 575ft; every 30 min, Apr-mid Jun 7.25am-5pm, mid Jun-mid Sept 8.25am-8.25pm*).

EXPLORING THE BAY OF NAPLES

Sorrento★★

The focus of the peninsula is **Sorrento★★**, a favoured holiday playground for much of the last 2 500 years. Astonishingly, with all that popularity, the town has not succumbed to over-indulgence and is still utterly charming. Facilities for tourists are supremely well-organised and everything stays open all year round. It is no wonder that this is the base of choice for the majority of tourists to the Bay of Naples.

Sorrento has one museum, the **Museo Correale di Terranova★**, a 17C villa housing an eclectic mix of Neapolitan landscape paintings, statuary, and 17C-18C furniture, china and glass. Other than that, there are a

The attractive harbour of Sorrento, a popular resort.

The Sorrentine Peninsula and Amalfi Coast

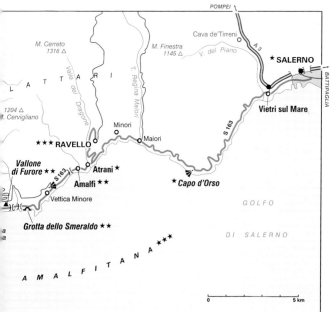

Not an inch of sand to be seen, on San Francesco Marina, Sorrento.

The bell tower of the Duomo, Sorrento.

few attractive churches but the real joy of the town is simply to stroll around the vibrant streets of the old town and hang out in the many pavement cafés.

Ferries dock in the **Marina Piccola**. Directly above it, the focal point of the town is **Piazza Tasso**, named after the local 16C poet, Torquato Tasso. Along the main road, Corso Italiano, are several interesting buildings including the 18C **Palazzo Correale**, with a fine majolica courtyard, and the 15C **Duomo**. Of the other churches, the most interesting is the **Chiesa di San Francesco** (Church of St Francis), which has a beautiful 13C Sicilian-Arab **cloister★**.

The cafés around the Piazza Tasso are favourites with tourists in summer.

Concerts are held in the cloister in summer. The nearby public gardens, **Villa Communale**, offer great **views★★** of the Bay of Naples.

At the base of the cliff, the old fishing port, the **Marina Grande**, is still a colourful hive of activity.

Capo di Sorrento

Tucked around Sorrento are several other pretty villages. **Sant'Agnello** and **Meta di Sorrento**, home to the 18C Bourbon shipyards, are effectively now residential suburbs. Meta has a noteworthy church, the **Basilica Santa Maria del Lauro**. **Piano di Sorrento** has a thriving market on Monday mornings. Perched high on the ridge of the Lattari mountains which form the backbone of the peninsula, **Sant'Agata sui Due Golfi** has superb **views★★** to the north, over the Bay of Naples, and the south, over the Gulf of Salerno. The far end of the peninsula belongs to **Massa Lubrense**, a scattering of 30 small hamlets hidden amongst breathtakingly lovely scenery, with excellent walks and superb views across to Capri.

COSTIERA AMALFITANA★★★
(THE AMALFI COAST)

There are no trains along the Amalfi Coast. Regular buses run from Naples, Sorrento and Salerno. Consider hiring a car for the day to allow you to stop and admire the views along the road. The 30km (19 mile) corniche along the southern coast of the Sorrentine peninsula is undoubtedly the most beautiful stretch of coast in Italy, a wild, tumbling landscape of mountains, cliffs, rocky coves and azure seas, adorned by several delightful historic towns, Saracen watch towers, tiny fishing hamlets, and long flights of narrow terraces nursing almonds and vines, olive and lemon trees.

It is an area beloved by artists, musicians and writers since Boccaccio used it as a setting for the *Decameron* (1349-53). It was in Positano that Diaghilev, Nijinsky, Picasso, Massine and Stravinsky laid the foundations of the greatest age of the Ballet Russe, while Nureyev later bought the tiny **Li Galli** islands, said to have been the home of the Sirens who sang sweetly to lure Odysseus onto the rocks. Franco Zeffirelli is only the latest of a list of international stars to find at least a temporary home here.

Positano★★★
Only one main road accessible to cars runs through the town and many hotels and apartments have no vehicle access. The elderly or disabled should be aware of potential problems when booking.

Positano★★★ underwent a boom period during the Amalfi Republic in the 9C-11C, and again in the 16C-17C when it was a trading centre to rival Venice. In 1953, John Steinbeck described it as having a population of about 2 000, with room for 500 tourists. He was confident that the geology of this virtually vertical town would halt development. It now has about 4 000 residents and 72 hotels.

There is only one real 'sight', the **Collegiata di Santa Maria Assunta** (Collegiate Church of St Mary of the Assumption), an imposing Baroque building with a brightly coloured majolica dome and a Byzantine icon of the Black Madonna. The town itself is the greatest attraction, a pyramid of sugar-cube fishermen's houses and lavish Baroque villas, leading down to a sandy beach brightened by gaily painted fishing boats.

Positano clings improbably to the hillside, with the dome of Santa Maria Assunta in the foreground.

Further along the coast, just beyond **Praiano**, another village growing in popularity as a resort is the **Vallone di Furore★★** (Furore Valley), a deep, steep-sided rocky gorge between two road tunnels. Unbelievably, a former fishing village nestles at the foot of the gorge, though the villas have been restored for holiday homes. Further on, through two more tunnels, the green **Grotta dello Smeraldo★★** (Emerald Grotto) is most interesting for its underwater stalactites, formed before the cave was drowned, and an extraordinary underwater crib (*accessible by lift or stairs from the road or by sea*).

Amalfi★★

Legend has it that **Amalfi★★** was founded by Roman citizens fleeing ahead of the Barbarian invasions. Whether or not this is true, it certainly retained links to the Byzantine Empire and was the first town in Italy to regroup in the 9C when it became the first of Italy's Maritime Republics. With a population of 70 000, it grew into one of Italy's leading cities, transforming itself into a Duchy in 958. This was the first city in the world to codify maritime law, in the 11C *Tavoli Amalfitane*, used until the 17C. It was crusaders from Amalfi who founded the Knights of St John. It was also the setting for Webster's powerful drama, the *Duchess of Malfi*. With a beautiful **setting★★★**, original architecture and mild climate, it is popular for day trips. **Via Genova** and **Via Capuano★** are the two main shopping streets, but visitors should take time to wander in the narrow alleys and passages leading off them, which reward the explorer with delightful unexpected little squares, often with pretty fountains.

The **Duomo di Sant'Andrea★** (Cathedral of St Andrew) was founded in the 9C and remodelled in the 11C. The magnificent golden mosaic façade was rebuilt in 1889-91, based on the Sicilian-Byzantine original. The bronze **doors★** were cast in Constantinople in 1065. In the crypt are the relics of the apostle, St Andrew, 'liberated' from Constantinople during the infamous 4th Crusade of 1204. To one side is the **Chiostro del Paradiso★★** (Cloister of Paradise), a serene Moorish-style cloister added in 1266-8 as an upmarket cemetery. The Cathedral also has a museum displaying its various treasures and artworks.

The striking Duomo di Sant'Andrea overlooks the lively Piazza Duomo, Amalfi.

Ravello★★★

*Regular buses run up the mountain from Amalfi.
For the energetic, the walk up involves about
1 200 steps. Most of the town is inaccessible to
motorised transport.*

If ever there were an enchanted village, this
is it, with its unforgettable **site★★★**, a clifftop
eyrie with superlative views, serene gardens,
and picture-book churches and villas.
Wagner used the gardens of the Villa Rufolo
as the model for the magic gardens of
Klingsor in *Parsifal* (1880). Not surprisingly,
Ravello attracted many artists, musicians and
writers, among them members of the
Bloomsbury Group (Virginia and Leo
Woolf), DH Lawrence, Graham Greene and

*Indulge in the
pleasure of beauty,
in a realm where
nature and art are
one.*

*The view from Villa
Rufolo Gardens.*

Gore Vidal.

The 11C **Duomo** has superb **bronze doors★**, cast by Barisanus da Trani in 1179. Inside are a magnificent 12C mosaic **ambo** showing Jonah being swallowed by a rather fanciful whale, and an even more fantastic mosaic **pulpit★★** (1272). A side chapel houses the blood of the town's patron saint, San Pantaleone, said to liquify miraculously every year, like that of San Gennaro in Naples. Next door, the cameo shop, **Camo** (*Piazza Duomo 9*) has a small museum of cameos and coral.

Shaded walks, marble busts and extensive panoramas are all on offer at Villa Cimbrone.

Opposite the cathedral, the **Villa Rufolo★★★** dates back to the 13C. This is the ancestral home of the area's most powerful family, but its formidable keep has since been tempered by an elegant courtyard and terraced gardens with fabulous **views★★★**. These terraces overlooking the sea provide a splendid setting for evening chamber music concerts (*April to August; special bus services from Amalfi and Sorrento*) and the Villa Rufolo hosts the Wagner Festival in July.

A charming, small, stepped **alley★** leads out from the town centre, past the twin churches of **San Francesco** (St Francis) and **Santa Chiara** (Church of St Clare) to the **Villa Cimbrone★★★**. In the late 19C, an Englishman, Lord Grimthorpe, transformed the house and created a fairy-tale garden, with shaded walkways, classical statuary, hidden arbours and a formal cliff-top terrace which provides an immense **panorama★★★** over terraced hillsides, Maiori, Cape Orso and the Gulf of Salerno.

THE SPIRIT OF NAPLES

The spirit of Naples inhabits the piazza, coated with marble columns and laced with jazzy café umbrellas, the air rich with a warm, luscious smell of pizza and fresh flowers, lemon, garlic, parmesan and coffee. All Neapolitan life is here. An elegant woman in a Max Mara suit and understated gold earrings teeters past with a small dog on a bright red lead. A teenage boy in black leather tries to look hip as he perches on his purple moped, smooths back hair shiny with gel, and leers lustfully at the mini-skirted girls. In the shadows, a fishmonger unerringly hurls a fish across to his customer for inspection. Snappy young men do a business deal, their mobile phones heaped between the cappuccinos. On the fountain steps

Enjoying a chat and a game of cards.

sprawls a group of backpackers in dirty jeans, sharing one ice-cream cone between four. Six policemen prowl past, tapping their guns. All of them, young and old, are wearing ultra-cool, black-framed, black-glass sunglasses …

It is not such a long journey from the ancient Greek agora or Roman forum to the modern piazza. People still come out to stroll the narrow streets, sip a leisurely aperitif, do business over bowls of pasta and catch up on the local gossip. Then Roman patricians arrived for seaside holidays in richly decorated villas, now American tourists clutching guidebooks head for lavishly appointed hotels. Emperor Augustus collected ancient Greek artefacts to decorate his villa. Now the museums proudly display ancient Roman remains. Where the Roman temple with its statues of Zeus and Aphrodite stood now stands a gilded Baroque church festooned with statues of Christian saints and martyrs. Life in Naples is young and trendy; it also goes back many centuries.

WEATHER

The climate here is as close to perfection as you can find in Europe. Winter can be changeable, but there is plenty of sunshine and the temperature is pleasant, rarely dropping below freezing.

The spring weather (mid Apr–early June) remains a little unpredictable, and it is still too cold to swim, but sunny days are warm and the early evenings balmy.

At the height of summer (Jul-Aug), the temperature rarely goes above 35°C (95°F), with long, sunny days and occasional tempestuous but short-lived thunder storms.

Autumn is probably perfect, slightly cooler but still hot and sunny, while the sea remains warm enough to swim. The official season usually ends in mid-October.

CALENDAR OF EVENTS

Dec-Jan *Inferno Sorrento* – a programme of events and concerts for winter tourists.

8 Dec – *Feast of the Immaculate Conception* marks the official start of the Christmas festivities.

24 Dec – Christmas Eve presents and feasting are followed by midnight mass.

31 Dec *New Year's Eve* – fireworks and frolics in the Piazza del Plebiscito, **Naples**.

6 Jan – *Epiphany* is celebrated by the arrival of the Befana witch in the Piazza del Plebiscito, **Naples**. Good children are given sweets; naughty ones get lumps of coal (actually sweets in the form of coal).

Feb *Mardi Gras Carnival* – everyone eats lasagne.

19 March *Feast of San Giuseppe* – with a bird festival in Via

ENJOYING YOUR VISIT

Medina, **Naples**; everyone eats doughnuts.

Last weekend March *3-day Cultural Festival* – museums open longer hours, with free or heavily discounted admission, smaller sights not usually open to the public fling wide their doors, and there are many special events and exhibitions.

Good Friday – various *penitential processions*, with the biggest on the island of Procida. In **Meta di Sorrento**, a series of processions retrace the events of the whole of Christ's Passion. A *torchlight procession* winds through the streets of Sorrento at 3am.

Easter Monday – a family day, with the restaurants full of celebratory parties. **Madonna dell'Arco**, (15km/9 miles) east of Naples, has a procession with flowery carts and a massive picnic.

May, 1st Sunday *Celebration of the Miracle of San Gennaro* – the saint's blood liquifies at the Duomo and his statue is carried in procession through **Naples**.

July-Sept *Estate a Napoli* – a 3-month cultural festival in **Naples**, with music, drama, performance art and film. Many other towns have summer *music festivals*. The *Wagner Festival* in **Ravello** attracts world-class performers; others worth looking out for include those at **Positano** and **Sorrento**.

July *Feast of the Madonna del Carmine* – celebrated in the Piazza Mercato, **Naples**, and Piazza Tasso, **Sorrento**.

26 July – illuminated boats and fireworks on **Ischia** for the *Feast of Sant'Anna*.

August – *The Landing of the Saracens* is reenacted in **Positano** with full costume and great enthusiasm.

September *Settembrata Anacaprese* – a month of games, competition and gastronomy in **Anacapri**.

19 September – second celebration of the miraculous blood of *San Gennaro*.

2 November *All Souls' Day* – everyone takes flowers to the family graves, then goes out for a slap-up meal.

ACCOMMODATION

There is a huge variety of accommodation available both in Naples and the surrounding area. Standards are generally high, with some of the finest **hotels** in Italy gracing the city waterfront, Capri and Sorrento. The bad news is that prices are high; expect to pay at least £35 (indicated as very inexpensive below) for a basic room without bath in a **pension** or 1* hotel, £35-55 (inexpensive) for a reasonable 2-3* hotel; £55-80 (moderate) for a good 3-4*; £80-120 (expensive) for a normal 4*, and anything up to £335 (very expensive) at the top end of the market. Accommodation is generally less expensive in smaller Italian towns, rising in Naples. Prices are per night, based on two people sharing, with bed and breakfast, in high season.

The official government classification ranges from 1* hotels providing the most basic facilities to 5* at the top of the range. Although the star ratings do give an indication of what facilities you can expect, they do not always reflect charm or ambience, and you may find a lower rated pension more than makes up in character for what it lacks in facilities.

Most tourists choose to stay on the Sorrentine Peninsula or the islands. Prices are lower here but can still mount up, while Capri adds a premium for its upmarket image. If you are planning to stay in the area for a week or more, the best bet is probably to look at what the package tours have to offer. Their ability to bulk buy will give you better accommodation for your budget, and with everything so close and accessible it is easy to do all your sightseeing from one base.

The **Associazione Italiana Alberghi per la Gioventù** is the Italian branch of the International Youth Hostel Federation. Although there are not many **youth hostels** in Italy, some are located in historic buildings. You will need an international membership card to book (available in the UK or in the hostels themselves). In Naples, the Ostello Mergellina (*Salita della Grotta 23*, ☎ 081-761 2346) is conveniently situated near the Mergellina station. Contact AIG at Via Cavour 44, 00184 Rome, ☎ 06 487 1152.

Other alternatives include **villa** or **apartment rental**, with a relatively small number of properties available. Contact:

Interhome

UK: *383 Richmond Rd, Twickenham, Middx TW1 2EF.* ☎ **0181-891 1294** Fax: 0181-891 5331. Web: www.interhome.com

USA: *1990 NE 163rd Street Suite 110, North Miami, Florida 33162.* ☎ **(305) 940 2299** Fax: (305) 940 2911

There are several well-placed

camping and caravan sites (*see* p.113).

A full list of all accommodation is available from tourist offices. For up-to-date information on hotels and restaurants, consult the *Michelin Red Guide Italia*. This guide, which is updated every year, offers a selection of hotels, from the simplest to the most luxurious, classified by district and according to comfort.

Recommendations

NAPLES
Lungomare
The seafront near the Castel dell'Ovo is lined by a row of the biggest and plushest hotels in Naples. Between them are scattered a few cheaper hotels and pensions of reasonable quality. This is undoubtedly the best area in which to stay if you can manage to get a room.

Santa Lucia *Via Partenope 46,* ☎ **081-764 0666**; Numero Verde (freephone) ☎ **167-887 014** Fax: 081-764 8580. After a facelift, this famous hotel is once more among the city's top hotels. Waft through halls filled with frescoes, elaborate stucco, Murano chandeliers and 18C antiques; dine at the wonderful *Megaris* restaurant (expensive).

Royal/Continental Hotels *Via Partenope 38/44,* ☎ **081-764 4800/764 4636** Fax: 081-764 5707/764 4661. Large, modern

and efficient, these joint hotels housing the city's largest hotel conference facilities are well set up for business travellers and perfectly situated on the seafront. Slightly less expensive than their older neighbours. Pool (expensive).

Miramare *Via Nazario Sauro 24,* ☎ **081-764 7589** Fax: 081-764 0775. The smallest (30 rooms) and most intimate of the upmarket hotels along the seafront, the Miramare is a delightfully restored Art Nouveau villa; roof garden and views of the Bay and Vesuvius (expensive).

Canada *Via Mergellina 43,* ☎ **081-680 952** Fax: 081-651 594. Simple but comfortable accommodation on the seafront in Mergellina. The bedrooms are reasonably sized, but the common rooms are tiny (inexpensive/moderate).

Ausonia *Via Caracciolo 11, Mergellina,* ☎ **081-682 278** Fax: 081-664 536. A short way back from the waterfront, in one wing of an old mansion block, this is one of the best budget hotels in town. Only 20 rooms, so book ahead and get confirmation in writing (inexpensive/very inexpensive).

Le Fontane al Mare *Via Niccolo Tommaseo 14,* ☎ **081-764 3811** Fax: 081-764 3470. Simple, friendly, cheap hotel, superbly located on the 4th floor of a mansion block on the seafront. Keep a L200 coin handy to work the lift (very inexpensive).

City Centre

Away from the seafront, there are some excellent hotels sprinkled around the shopping district of Via Chiaia and the Centro Storico (old town), within walking distance of many of the top sights, shops and restaurants.

Mercure Angioino *Via Depretis 123*, ☎ **081-552 9500** Fax: 081-552 9509. A relatively new addition to the city, run by the well-known French chain, this fine hotel provides all the amenities, in an excellent location between Castel Nuovo and Spaccanapoli (moderate).

Pinto-Storey *Via Martucci 72*, ☎ **081-681 260** Fax: 081-667 536. Charming small 3rd floor hotel, right next to the Piazza Amedeo, with antiques in the hall and friendly service (moderate).

Hotel Suite Esedre *Via Cantani 12*, ☎ **081-553 7087**. One of the newest and best-regarded cheaper hotels in the old town area (inexpensive).

Near the Station

The area around the main station is always a good hunting ground for cheap hotels and Naples is no exception. Unfortunately, the Piazza Garibaldi and its side roads have become one of the roughest areas in the city and it is not safe to walk around here alone at night. Unless price is your only consideration, look elsewhere.

Grand Hotel Terminus *Piazza*

It's impossible to avoid steps when exploring the streets of Positano.

Garibaldi, ☎ **081-286 011** Fax: 081-206 689. A fine old hotel, built in 1919 and totally restored within the last few years. The facilities are good, but it suffers from an appalling location (expensive).

Casanova *Via Venezia 2*, ☎ **081-268 287** Fax: 081-269 792. One of the better small, cheap hotels near the station, for those who feel compelled to stay in the area (very inexpensive).

Vomero/Capodimonte

Those who prefer to be a short way from the madding crowd may prefer the leafy hills above the city centre.

Britannique *Corso Vittorio*

Emanuele 133, ☎ **081-761 4145**
Fax: 081-660 457. This grand old
hotel is a Neapolitan institution,
the imposing 19C building set in
lush gardens, with superb views.
Old-fashioned elegance and
seamless service (moderate).

THE SORRENTINE COAST

This is *the* centre of tourist accommodation on the mainland, with
around 120 hotels, most of them
well-situated and well-run. There
are good hotels in towns such as
Vico Equense, but they tend to
act as overflows for when

*Hotel and outdoor restaurant on
Via Camerelle, Capri.*

Sorrento itself is full. For
charming country hotels, look in
Massa Lubrense, where numerous
delightful places at relatively low
prices offer fabulous views,
gardens, pools and local walks.

Sorrento
Grand Hotel Excelsior Vittoria
Piazza T. Tasso 34, ☎ **081-807
1044**; Numero Verde: 1678-90053
Fax: 081-877 1206. On the main
square (with a private lift down to
the port), the Excelsior Vittoria,
opened in 1834, is probably the
most famous landmark in
Sorrento. Always owned by the
same family, it has played host to
notables from Goethe to Caruso
and Marylin Monroe. Elegantly
decorated with frescoes and
antiques, its gardens festooned
with wisteria, it is a haven of old-
fashioned elegance. Pool and
restaurant (very expensive).
Grand Hotel Royal *Via Correale
42,* ☎ **081-807 3434** Fax: 081-877
2905. Another imposing 19C cliff-
top hotel, this is less spectacular
but still extremely comfortable.
Several package operators offer
stays within reach of normal
budgets. Sun terrace, pool and
views of Vesuvius (expensive).
The same management has three
other good hotels: the Ambascia-
tori, Capodimonte and Hotel de
la Ville.
Villa di Sorrento *Piazza Tasso,
Via Fuorimura 6,* ☎ **081-878 1068**
Fax: 081-878 0372. Pleasant small

hotel which makes up for the lack of a sea view by its perfect position right in the town centre. The rooms are simple but comfortable and the price very attractive (inexpensive).

Hotel Loreley et Londres *Via Califano 2,* ☎/Fax: **081-807 3187**. A true bargain. This cliff-top mansion has been converted to a simply but attractively furnished hotel with a pool, a lift to the seafront and fabulous sea views (very inexpensive).

Youth Hostel *Via degli Aranci 160,* ☎ **081-807 2925** (very inexpensive).

Outside Sorrento

La Badia *Via Nastro Verde 8,* ☎ **081-878 1154** Fax: 081-807 4159. A real find, this delightful little hotel is a converted abbey, set amidst olive and lemon groves on the hill just above Sorrento (on the bus route to the centre; 10 min), with superb views over the town and bay. Attractively furnished, friendly, with a pool and restaurant (inexpensive).

CAPRI

La Scalinatella *Via Tragara 8,* ☎ **081-837 0633** Fax: 081-837 8291. Immaculately luxurious small hotel whose 30 rooms all have jacuzzis, balconies and sea views. White walls and arches form a perfect backdrop to opulent oriental furniture. Pool (very expensive).

Villa Sarah *Via Tiberio 3/a,* ☎ **081-837 7817** Fax: 081-837 7215. Peaceful whitewashed hotel (20 rooms) with shady gardens set amidst the vineyards on the outskirts of Capri town. 20 rooms (moderate).

Villa Krupp *Via Matteoti 12,* ☎ **081-837 0362** Fax: 081-837 6489. On the cliff-top overlooking the Marina Piccola, this historic villa was once home to Lenin and Gorky. With only 12 rooms and bargain prices, the no-frills, family-run hotel is one of the most popular options on Capri. Book ahead (inexpensive).

ISCHIA

Miramare *Via Comandante Maddalena 29, Sant'Angelo,* ☎ **081-999 219** Fax: 081-999 325. Pretty, quiet and secluded hotel with a terrace and panoramic views over the small harbour (moderate).

La Villarosa *Via Giacinto Gigante 5, Ischia Porto,* ☎ **081-991 316** Fax: 081-992 425. This town centre hotel has 37 rooms and charming sitting rooms, all lovingly furnished with 19C antiques. The lush terraced garden surrounds a thermal pool (inexpensive).

Il Monastero *Castello Aragonese, Ischia Ponte,* ☎ **081-992 435**. The rooms of this former monastery are almost spartan, but prices are cheap and the setting, inside the castle walls, and views are fabulous (very inexpensive).

AMALFI COAST
Amalfi

Luna Convento *Via P Comite 33,* ☎ **089-871 002** Fax: 089-871 333. This glorious hotel is housed in a Saracen tower and a 13C medieval monastery, about 5 min walk uphill from the cathedral. Owned and managed by the same family since 1825, this is Amalfi's oldest and probably most popular hotel. Pool and sea views (expensive).

La Bussola *Lungomare dei Cavalieri 1,* ☎ **089-871 533** Fax: 089-871 369. A friendly, family-run hotel in a converted mill, with simple rooms and sea views from the terrace (inexpensive).

Lido Mare *Largo Ducci Piccolomene 9,* ☎ **089-871 332** Fax: 089-871 394. Pretty little whitewashed hotel, with simple furnishings and cool Moorish arches. Some rooms have sea views (very inexpensive).

Positano

Villa Franca e Residence *Viale Pasitea 318,* ☎ **089-875 655** Fax: 089-875 735. Charmingly designed, cool and tranquil hotel just above the town centre. All rooms have views of the town and sea, many have private balconies. Pool (expensive).

Casa Albertina *Via della Tavolozza 3,* ☎ **089-875 143** Fax: 089-811 540. Small, friendly and attractive town centre hotel. Views of the coast from the rooms and rooftop

terrace restaurant (moderate).

Maria Luisa *Via Fornillo 40,* ☎/Fax: **089-875 023**. Cheap, friendly pension with 10 rooms (very inexpensive).

Youth Hostel *Via G. Marconi 358,* ☎ **089-875 857** (very inexpensive).

Ravello

Villa Cimbrone *Via Santa Chiara 26,* ☎ **089-858 072** Fax: 089-857 777. One of Ravello's top tourist attractions. The house was given a new lease of life in the 19C from a 12C original. The furnishings are magnificent; previous guests have included EM Forster and Greta Garbo. The gardens and view are some of Italy's finest (expensive).

Villa Maria *Via Santa Chiara 2,* ☎ **089-857 255** Fax: 089-857 071. A carefully restored villa, rich with antiques, a short walk from the town centre, with a stunning terrace and lush gardens (expensive). Next door, and owned by the same family, is the larger, more modern, cheaper **Hotel Giordano**. Shared pool and other facilities.

Villa Amore *Via dei Fusco,* ☎ **089-857 135** Fax: 089-857 135. Tucked away from the road in shady gardens, with cliff-top views, this converted villa (14 rooms) offers all the luxuries of location, together with simple furnishings, friendly service and a great price tag (very inexpensive).

FOOD AND DRINK

Food

While pizza is king (*see* p.99), there is much, much more to Neapolitan cuisine. The food here largely has peasant origins – it is hearty and designed to fill and satisfy at low cost. These days, of course, many of these simple dishes have become very trendy, with a price tag to match.

Mozzarella is present on every menu, often simply served as a large lump of cheese, but sometimes fried and with an endless variety of sauces. Most restaurants have an astonishing array of grilled and marinated vegetables as *antipasti*. **Seafood** (*frutti di mare*) is ever present, with salads, pastas, risottos and soups all made from clams, shrimps and other shellfish. Simply grilled or fried white fish, with a light sauce, is a popular main course.

Naples claims to be the original home of **spaghetti**, which is usually served with a tomato sauce, with a meat and tomato *ragù*, or *alla parmigiana* (with aubergines, tomato and cheese). Heavy winter soups come laden with pasta, beans and green vegetables (*pasta e fagioli*). On Capri and the Sorrentine Peninsula, rabbit is a popular meat dish, and residents have devised an imaginative variety of ways of cooking this locally abundant creature.

The calendar is punctuated by

a series of different **cakes and pastries** designed to meet the needs of each new holiday. The *pastiera* is a ubiquitous Easter tart, with a pastry base and filling of buttermilk curd and corn. Christmas is greeted by *strùffoli*, pastries stuffed with honey and fruit, while the feast of San Giuseppe merits *zeppole* (similar to ring doughnuts). For those needing a lighter touch, the city produces some of Italy's (and the world's) finest ice-creams.

Drink

While Italy is one of the largest

wine producers in the world and Campania does have vineyards, none of the local labels are in anyway outstanding. The most famous is *Lacryma Christi* (Tears of Christ), a sweet white wine grown on the slopes of Mt Vesuvius. *Greco di Tufo* is a good local dry white wine. Other local wines, which have a distinctive slightly sulphurous taste, include Capri (red and white), Ischia (white) and Gragnano (red).

The real speciality of the area is *Limoncello*, a wonderful **liqueur** made from lemon peel and which is drunk icy cold, straight from the freezer.

Eating Out

Eating is a passion in Italy, and Italian food is one of the major pleasures awaiting tourists. Allow plenty of time to enjoy long, leisurely meals, often in superb surroundings.

Breakfast is simple, usually only milky coffee and a croissant, although the larger hotels serve a buffet with fruit, cereal, cheese and other options. Traditionally, the main meal of the day is eaten at lunchtime, although this is changing as the country slowly falls into line with standard office hours elsewhere in Europe. Options for a light **lunch** include pizza and filled rolls (*panini*), from a range of delicatessens and bakeries as well as bars and trattorie.

The full **main meal** starts with *antipasti*, a selection of (usually) cold, marinated vegetables, meats or fish, followed by the *primo* (first course), usually a plate of pasta or risotto. Vegetables or salad must be ordered separately from the *secundo* (second course) of fish or meat, which comes without any accompaniment. Those who still have room can top it off with dessert, coffee and a digestif.

There is relatively little difference between eating establishments these days but, technically, the finest restaurants are called **ristorante**, while smaller, less formal neighbourhood restaurants are **trattoria**. **Pizzerias** are for pizza, though most serve other things as well. Opening hours are from 12.30-3.30pm, and 8pm-midnight. Expect to pay up to L25 000 for an inexpensive meal, L20-50 000 in the middle range and over L50 000 in the expensive category, for a full meal for one, without wine. There will always be a cover charge simply for sitting down. Service charges are included, but a small additional tip is customary.

Part of the fun is wandering through the streets, building up an appetite, comparing menus and waiting for one to take your fancy, but a few suggestions are given below, together with price indications.

Pizza

Of all the marvellous creations in Naples, the most famous must be the humble pizza, whose popularity has spread around the globe – although now laden with extraordinary additions, from pineapple to chicken tikka, that no self-respecting Neapolitan would recognise.

The pizza began life as far back as the Neolithic Period, when a flour and water dough was rolled out and cooked on hot stones. It was certainly eaten at Pompeii, where a statue of a pizza vendor was found in the ruins.

The familiar dough base is a typical yeast-leaven Mediterranean flat bread, similar to *pitta*, seasoned with cheese or other ingredients. Buffalo were brought south by the Lombards in the early Middle Ages, and from them came a now near staple ingredient, mozzarella cheese, famously elastic (and difficult to eat politely!) when melted. The tomato was introduced by the Spanish, who brought it back from South America in the 16C. It was initially considered poisonous (it is a cousin of deadly nightshade), but its use spread in Italy in the mid-18C, when it

was regarded as an aphrodisiac.

By the early 17C, the name pizza had been coined, and by the mid-18C, vendors roamed the streets of Naples with tin ovens balanced on their heads to keep the pizzas warm. It was rapidly becoming a standard meal at all levels of society. In the early 20C, the pizza emigrated, with the first being sold in the United States in 1905.

Today, a proper Neapolitan pizza must have a thin, crispy base, with the dough thrown rather than rolled, a thin coating of other ingredients (the deep pan is an American aberration) and be cooked in a wood-fired oven. In 1889, the simple but delicious combination of olive oil, tomato, mozzarella and basil (the colours of the Italian flag) was officially named the *Pizza Margherita*, in honour of Queen Margherita of Italy. It has become the classic pizza topping.

Recommendations

NAPLES
Restaurants
Lungomare

Some of the finest restaurants in this area are in the palace hotels (see above).

Ciro a Mergellina *Via Mergellina 18-21,* ☎ **081-681 780**.
The lack of a sea view is the only thing wrong with this spacious restaurant, whose buffets, seafood, pastas and pizzas are all mouthwatering. Other branches of the restaurant are in the Borgo Marinaro and Via Santa Brigida (expensive; closed Mon; Fri in summer).

Ristorante La Bersagliera *Borgo Marinaro 10/11,* ☎ **081-764 6016**.
Finest of the restaurants surrounding the now trendy old fishermen's quarter around the Castel dell'Ovo, with great views of the castle and yachts. The food adds a light modern twist to classic Neapolitan recipes, with wonderful fish and vegetables. Open terrace in summer. Booking advisable (expensive; closed Tues).

Pizzeria Brandi *Salita S. Anna di Palazzo 1/2 (corner of Via Chiaia),* ☎ **081-416 928**. Something of a tourist trap these days, but it is almost impossible to visit Naples without paying homage to the place that invented the *Pizza Margherita* in 1889. The pizzas are still excellent and the atmosphere convivial (moderate).

Osteria del Castello *Via S. Teresa a Chiaia, 38,* ☎ **081-440 486**.
A charming, cheap little osteria in a side street near the Piazza Amedeo. The short menu of chef's specials changes daily according to what is available, but the results are always good and the family atmosphere is friendly (inexpensive).

Vini e Cucina *Corso Vittorio Emanuele 762,* ☎ **081-660 302**.
Cheerful, basic home cooking in a busy trattoria near Mergellina station (inexpensive; closed Sun; Aug 20-30).

Centro Storico (Old Town)
La Cantinella *Via Cuma 42,* ☎ **081-764 8684**.
Power lunch 'see and be seen' restaurant, with fabulous views from the terrace. The food is good, but the atmosphere better (very expensive).

Pizzeria Bellini *Via Santa Maria di Costantinopoli 79/80,* ☎ **081-459 774**. One of the city's longest-established and most famous restaurants, with excellent pizzas and pastas. Try the signature *linguine al cartoccio*. Outdoor terrace (moderate; closed Sun).

Osteria dell'Arte *Via Rampe SG Maggiore 1/a,* ☎ **081-552 7558**.
Cosy old town inn. Amongst the usual pastas lurk traditional Neapolitan tavern favourites, such as hearty vegetable soups or tripe and onions, designed to

temper the effects of an evening's hard drinking. Limited space, so book ahead (moderate; closed Sun; Aug).

Pizzeria da Michele *Via Cesare Sersale 1-3*, ☎ **081-553 9204**. In the Forcella district, next to the historic centre; noisy, basic and cheap, with shared tables, a lively atmosphere and some of the finest pizzas in Naples. Only two flavours – *margherita* or *marinara*. Come early (inexpensive; closed Sun; 12 days in Aug).

Trattoria Palumbo Gennaro *Via S. Chiara 6*. Basic neighbourhood restaurant serving a limited menu of good, simple meals. Very cheap, and ideally placed for a lunch stop, just off the Piazza del Gèsu in the old town (inexpensive).

Posillipo
Giuseppone a Mare *Via Ferdinando Russo 13, Posillipo*, ☎ **081-575 6002**. Classic cuisine – Campanian specialities and seafood – and a fabulous location and view make this justly one of the most famous and sought after restaurants in the city (expensive; closed Wed; Sun in summer; 7 days in Aug).

Cafés and Bars
Gran Caffè Gambrinus *Piazza Trieste e Trento*. The most glamorous and historic café in the city, founded in 1866, this glorious haven of ladies in hats is still redolent of 19C high society. There is a take-away section for those who want the cakes without the white linen and silver service.

Intra Moenia *Piazza Bellini 70*. Popular intellectual hangout in the old town. This combined café and bookshop also hosts occasional cultural events.

Gelateria della Scimmia *Piazza Carità 4*. Ice-cream to die for, made on the premises.

Dizzy Club *Corso Vittorio Emanuele 19-20*. A dizzying array of 150 cocktails. Cards and chess are available as alternative entertainment (open 8pm-2am; closed Wed).

Internet Bar *Piazza Bellini 74*. For those seriously addicted to surfing the net (open daily 11am-2am).

POMPEII
La Locanda di Annagrazia *Via Colle S Bartolomeo 71* ☎ **081-863 25 05**. Small and typical Italian inn, friendly atmosphere and rustic decor, serving traditional cuisine. Try its *Antipasti assortito*, a meal in itself, with a bottle of Greco di Tufo or a jug of local red wine grown on the slopes of Vesuvius.

THE SORRENTINE COAST
Restaurants
Sorrento
La Fenice *Via degli Aranci 11*, ☎ **081-878 1652**. One of the best restaurants in Sorrento, built like a conserva-

tory and bedecked with flowers. The long, largely traditional menu that ranges from pizza to flambés does have a few surprises, such as black noodles with courgette flowers and shrimps, to liven it up (expensive).

La Lanterna Mare *Via Marina Grande 44,* ☎ **081-807 3033**. Silver service, delicious seafood, a mouth-watering dessert trolley and a waterfront setting in the Marina Grande. Wonderful (expensive).

La Lanterna *Via S. Cesareo 23/25,* ☎ **081-878 1355**.

Sit back, relax and watch the cheerful Italian family parties at this excellent old town restaurant and pizzeria.

A few outdoor tables. Owned by the same people as the Lanterna Mare (moderate).

Trattoria da Emilia *Via Marina Grande 62,* ☎ **081-807 2720**. Small, family-run trattoria on the seafront, serving a limited menu of simply cooked fresh fish and pasta. Wooden tables, check cloths, candles in bottles and family photos on the wall. Very, very popular (inexpensive; closed Tues).

The Chez Black, Positano.

Cafés and Bars
Bar Ercolano *Piazza Tasso.*
Delightful outdoor café/bar,
right in the centre of the main
square, perfectly placed for
people-watching on balmy
evenings.
Bar Primavera *Via Fuorimuro
20/Corso Italia 142* . Cheerful,
busy old town bar and coffee
shop, with everything from whisky
to sticky cakes and ice-cream on
offer.
**Circolo dei Forestieri (Foreign-
ers' Club)** *Via L. De Maio 35.* This
extraordinary institution has a
huge, magnificent cliff-top
terrace, with some of the best
views in Sorrento, live music most
evenings, drinks (from tea to
cocktails) and snacks almost
round the clock, and a full menu
at mealtimes.

OUTSIDE SORRENTO
Restaurants
Don Alfonso *Sant'Agata sui due
Golfi,* ☎ **081-878 0026.** Considered by many to be the best
restaurant south of Rome, this
tiny establishment has won
international acclaim for its
magnificent cuisine using fresh
local produce (the olive oil and
vegetables are grown by the pro-
prietors), and its superb cellar.
Light, floral decor, and friendly
well-informed staff. Go into
training for the 'degustation'
menu. There are a few bedrooms
(very expensive; booking essen-

tial; closed Mon; Mon-Tues in
winter; Jan 17-Feb 27).
Antico Franceschiello da Peppino
Via Partenope 27, Massa Lubrense,
☎ **081-533 9780.** Long-established, entertaining family-run
restaurant serving traditional
food, including a sumptuous
buffet, in a wonderful setting.
Inside, the walls are covered in
local ceramics, outside is a
superlative view across the bay
(moderate; closed Wed in
winter).

THE ISLANDS
Restaurants
Capri
Da Paolino *Via Palazzo a Mare 11,
Marina Grande,* ☎ **081-837 6102.**
Pretty restaurant set among the
lemon groves and relying heavily
on their produce in its deft
antipasti, grilled fish and mouth-
watering desserts (expensive;
book ahead; closed Feb-Easter;
Tues in low season; lunchtime
Jun-Sept).
Canzone del Mare *Via Marina
Piccola 93, Marina Piccola,* ☎ **081-
837 0104.** The ritziest lunch on
the island. Sip white wine sangria
on an outdoor terrace, in the
company of jet-setting regulars.
The food is worthy of the
ambience (expensive; book
ahead; open Apr-Oct, lunch
only).
Aurora *Via Fuorlovado 18, Capri,*
☎ **081-837 0181.** Celebrity photos
line the walls, but the pizzas are

just as famous at this long-established and highly popular pizzeria (expensive; closed Jan-Mar).

Ischia

Damiano *Via Nuova Circumvallazione, Ischia Porto,* ☎ **081-983 032**. Fabulous seafood and a panoramic view of the port, all washed down with southern Italian wines (expensive; open Apr-Sept, dinner only, except Sun).

Da Peppina di Renato *Via Bocca 42, Forio,* ☎ **081-998 312**. Typical island trattoria serving good country cooking, with ingredients so fresh they are practically still walking. Outdoor terrace with sea views (moderate; open Mar-Nov; closed lunchtimes and Wed, except Jun-Sept).

AMALFI COAST
Restaurants
Amalfi

La Caravella *Via Matteo Camera 12,* ☎ **089-871 029**. The food more than makes up for the lack of decor in this imaginative restaurant, where the local seafood and citrus are kings. Leave room for the wonderful desserts. Limited places; book ahead (expensive; closed Tues, except in Aug; all Nov).

Trattoria Da Gemma *Via Frà Gerardo Sasso 9,* ☎ **089-871 345**. An old-established Amalfi favourite, with a pleasing outdoor terrace and delicious seafood spe-

cialities. Book ahead (expensive; closed Wed, except in summer; all Aug).

Positano

La Cambusa *Piazza A. Vespucci,* ☎ **089-875 432**. This is probably Positano's premier restaurant, frequented by the great and the good. Put on some sparkle and feast on succulent seafood at outdoor tables with splendid views. Book ahead (expensive; closed 7-30 Jan).

Chez Black *Via Brigantino 19,* ☎ **089-875 036**. Harbourside restaurant and pizzeria with a terrace leading straight onto the beach (*see* p.102). The pizzas are excellent, but the seafood pasta is better and the ice-cream sundaes are calorific heaven (moderate; closed 7 Jan-7 Feb).

Ravello

Cumpà Cosimo *Via Roma 44-46,* ☎ **089-857 156**. Cheerful, busy sidestreet trattoria that is everyone's favourite stop. Go into training for the signature *piatti misto di primi,* a vast plate of half a dozen different types of pasta (moderate; closed Mon from Nov-Mar).

SHOPPING
Fashion

The Italians are very style conscious, and Naples, Sorrento and Capri are full of top name designer boutiques, at affordable prices. For the best selection, try the **Chiaia** district in Naples, the **Corso Italia** in Sorrento, or **Capri** town centre. **Positano** has become something of a small-scale fashion centre, with several new designers spreading their wings here. Some are happy to custom design and make clothes up for you. Leather jackets, bags and designer spectacles are other good buys, and leather sandals can be custom-made.

The islands and Sorrento Peninsula have small-scale perfume industries, with light, flowery scents based on local wildflowers and citrus.

Food

There is something superlative about shopping in an Italian street market – the only problem is getting things home at the end of your holiday. Limoncello, olives, olive oil, salted capers, salamis, sun-dried tomatoes, home-made tomato purées and pesto sauces, dried porcini (mushrooms), herbs and spices, fresh parmesan and other cheeses all make excellent souvenirs and gifts. If you prefer them in elegant bottles, jars and boxes, the delis have an enticing selection. Try the **Spaccanapoli** district of Naples on a Sunday morning,

Fruit stall in a Naples street.

when the street stalls are out and the whole local populace is on parade. In Amalfi, stop at the Pasticceria coloniale, Piazza Duomo, to taste and buy some **limoni** or **arance canditi** (candied orange and lemon).

Jewellery

A number of local jewellers produce vastly expensive designs for a jetset clientele. The real specialities of the region are **coral** and **cameos**, both of which are enormously beautiful but an ecological disaster. With the Mediterranean running out of shells and coral, the seas of the developing world are being stripped to keep the industry going. As a less harmful alternative, look at some of the costume jewellery made from spectacularly coloured volcanic rock.

Woodwork

For centuries, **Sorrento** has specialised in intricately inlaid marquetry furniture. These days, the very wealthy can still buy elaborate cupboards, tables and chests, but most of us are looking at the prospect of a musical box or tray. Some are beautiful, some tacky and poorly made, so shop around before buying.

Presepi

The *presepio* (Christmas crib) is not in itself a Neapolitan invention, but grew out of a medieval tradition found throughout Europe. The difference is that while most people have remained content to have a small nativity scene, only the *santons* of Provence, in France, show the same dedication to detail. The Neapolitans have raised the *presepio* to an art form, a symbol of the city, and a highly competitive business.

The first mention of *presepi* in the Naples region was in 1025. For centuries, they remained relatively simple – the familiar stable with Mary, Joseph, Jesus, a few sheep and cows, a shepherd or two and some wise men. By the mid-16C, there was a break with the medieval tradition, the cast began to grow and the first modern-dress versions were appearing. The golden age was during the reign of King Charles III, in the mid-18C, and many of the elaborate scenes created today still depict Bourbon Naples. The finest historic collection is in the Museo Nazionale di San Martino (*see* p.44).

Most are made of terracotta, but there are versions in wood, *papier maché*, plaster and even coral. What is important is the detail. Alongside the Holy Family, the cast of thousands will usually include musicians, beggars – some deformed or crippled – Ottoman Turks, and somewhere in the background a Roman ruin. The life of town, including all its crafts and shops, is lovingly displayed.

The crafting of *presepi* is

Making Capodimonte pottery.

traditionally a family affair, with workshops handed down through the generations. Many are clustered along Via San Gregorio Armeno, in the **Spaccanapoli** area of the old town (*see* p.5), together with numerous shops selling charming puppets and dolls.

Ceramics

The streets are full of brightly coloured and often very witty pottery, ranging from tiles to mugs, platters and huge pots and urns. Prices are reasonable and the selection endless. The finest selection is in the little town of **Vietri**, near Amalfi, where much of the pottery is made.

Antiques

Naples is renowned for its antiques trade, with excellent shops in or around Via Domenico Morelli. The *Fiera Antiquaria Napoletana* is an antiques market held on the penultimate weekend of each month, at the Villa Comunale. For the full annual programme of antique fairs, contact the tourist office. Remember to check whether you need permission to export your purchase.

ENTERTAINMENT AND NIGHTLIFE

Naples has the sort of nightlife that suits a former capital, port, university town, tourist resort and all-round major city – the place is jumping with something to suit every taste and pocket. The tourist office magazine, *Qui Napoli*, has excellent monthly listings, while details are available in the local daily paper, *Il Mattino*. The surrounding resorts also have above-average offerings, with an array of concerts, festivals and clubs. There are two general ticket agencies:

Box Office
Galleria Umberto I ☎ **081-551 9188**
Concerteria
Via M Schipa 23 ☎ **081-761 1221**

Music and Drama

In addition to the theatre productions by national and international companies through-out the year, which make Naples one of Italy's leading cities for **theatre**, there are various interna-tional festivals held in the region during the summer. Of course, the **Teatro San Carlo** (*Via San Carlo 93/f,* ☎ **081-797 2331**) is one of the great opera houses of the world, with a magnificent resident company (season from Dec-May). It also hosts tours by international ballet and opera companies and concerts. The box office is open Tues-Sun 10am-1pm, 4.30-6.30pm.

There are eight other theatres which offer concerts and drama, from the traditional to avant garde. Check at the tourist office for what's on.

There are two multiplex **cinemas** in the city centre: **Multicinema Modernissimo** (*Via Cisterna dell'Olio 59*, ☎ **081-551 1247**) and **Plaza Multisala** (*Via Kerbaker 85*, ☎ **081-556 3555**). Seats are cheaper on Wednesdays. All films are dubbed into Italian.

Naples has a buzzing nightlife, and **clubs, bars and discos** stay open into the early hours. You can hear live music at various spots in the city. **Riot** (*Via S Biagio dei Librai 39*) is a popular, loud, alternative multimedia club that also has exhibitions and live concerts. **Otto Jazz Club** (*Salita Cariati 23, Corso V. Emanuele*, ☎ **081-552 4373**) puts on a wide-ranging variety of jazz and blues for aficionados. **Bar dell'Ovo** (*Via Partenope 6*, ☎ **081-764 4280**) is an agreeably relaxed bar on the waterfront with great views and live piano music on Friday, Saturday and Sunday evenings. **Lido Pola** (*Via Nisida 34, Posillipo*, ☎ **081-571 1950**) offers dancing under the stars, with live music on some nights.

The main **amusement park** in Naples is **Edenlandia** (*Viale JF Kennedy*, ☎ **081-239 4090**). More for the children, it has over 200 attractions, based on traditional fables and Walt Disney favourites, but few spectacular rides that will appeal to teenagers and adults.

Ercolano
For details of the theatre productions in the ruins ☎ **081-850 6498** Fax: 081-850 7809.

Sorrento
Cinemas
Armida *Corso Italia 119*, ☎ 081-878 1470
Delle Rose *Via delle Rose, Piano di Sorrento*, ☎ **081-878 6165**
Clubs/ Discos
Fauno Notte Club *Piazza Tasso 1*, ☎ **081-878 1021**
La Mela Due *Corso Italia 263*, ☎ **081-878 4052**

The Amalfi Coast
Music and Drama
Villa Rufolo, *Ravello*. For details of the concerts held at the villa, contact Società dei Concerti di Ravello ☎ **089-85 81 49** Fax: 089-85 82 249, or the Tourist Office in Ravello ☎ **089-85 70 96** Fax: 089-85 79 77.
Clubs
Africana *Via Torre a Mare, Praiano*, ☎ **089-874 042**. The trendiest nightspot on the coast, this famous club is based in a cave, reached by a cliff path, with a

glass dance floor extending out over the sea.

Torre Saracena *Amalfi*, ☎ **089-871 084**. Set in a Saracen tower, just outside Amalfi.

SPORT

Of all their many passions, Neapolitan men reserve their greatest reverence for **football**, putting it almost on a par with religion. The city team, *Napoli*, plays at the Stadio San Paolo (☎ **081-239 5623**). The *Gran Premio* **trotting races** are held at the Ippodromo di Agnano race track (☎ **081-5701660**), about 10km (6 miles) outside the city every April, while the bay plays host to the *Vela Longa*, **a sailing regatta**, open to all.

Most of the larger hotels either have their own gym or provide guests with access to a city **health club**, of which there are plenty,

although only a few will take temporary members. There is a full list of sporting facilities in *Qui Napoli*.

All the towns in the region have public access **tennis courts** and there are superb **walks**, for example on the Sorrentine Peninsula or in the Craters degli Astroni nature reserve on Vesuvius. The weather makes **water sports** immensely popular here. Those unfortunate without a hotel pool can easily find a public one, while the sea is positively welcoming between mid-May and September. There is **scuba diving** from Capri and Positano; **sailing**, **canoeing** and **windsurfing** are available almost everywhere.

Taking the plunge, Sorrento.

THE BASICS

Before You Go

Everyone needs a valid **passport**, with the exception of EU citizens, who need only a national ID card for entry, if they have one. By law, people must carry their ID cards or passports at all times.

Visas are not required by any citizens of the EU, Commonwealth or the USA for stays of up to three months. Other nationalities should check with their nearest embassy or consulate before travelling.

No **vaccinations** are necessary. Italy has **reciprocal medical cover** with all EU member states and with Australia. UK citizens should fill out form E111, available over post office counters, and take this with them. It is strongly advised that all travellers should also take out comprehensive **travel insurance** to cover medical and other emergencies.

Getting There

By Air

There are direct scheduled services to Naples Capodichino airport from London, Paris, Brussels and Athens, along with a good network of domestic flights from main Italian cities. Most international scheduled services are routed via Rome or Milan. There are regular charter flights throughout the tourist season.

From the UK, the only scheduled operator to fly direct is **British Airways, ☎ 0345 222111** The cheapest option by air is to fly to Rome with **Go** (Central Booking ☎ **0845 605 4321**; website: www.go-fly.com), from London Stansted to Rome Ciampino, with easy onward rail connections.

Naples Capodichino airport (☎ **081-789 6111**) is about 10min drive from the city centre. There are airport buses into Naples and Sorrento, and local buses no 14 and 14r connect to Piazza Garibaldi. Taxis are plentiful.

Airline addresses in Naples
Alitalia: Via Medina 41
☎ **081-542 5111**
British Airways: Airport
☎ **081-789 6259**
Numero verde: **1478-12266**
Air France: Airport
☎ **081-789 6409**
KLM: Via S. Bartolomeo 63
☎ **081-552 3447**
Lufthansa: Piazza Municipio 72
☎ **081-551 5440**
TWA: Via Partenope 23
☎ **081-764 5828**

By Train

The national rail company, **Ferrovie dello Stato** (FS) runs excellent and very affordable rail connections with the rest of Italy, with some international services connecting via Milan or Rome.

Services from Rome Termini leave at least once an hour. The price rises steeply between the stopping services (about 3hrs) and the EC (Eurocity) and IC (Intercity) express trains (under 2hrs). Reservations are essential for EC trains; Interail passengers must pay a supplement.

Validate your ticket in the machine at the platform entrance before boarding.

The main station in Naples is the **Stazione Centrale**, Piazza Garibaldi; information ☎ 1478-88088 (numero verde; open 7am-9pm). Many of the trains from Rome also stop at **Campi Flegrei** and **Mergellina**.

By Coach

Coach services connect with all other major cities in Italy, and even a few international routes, such as the London-Naples direct service by National Express Eurolines (☎ 0582 404511).

By Car

Italy has an extensive network of toll motorways for speedy inter-city journeys. Credit cards are accepted for payment. A fast 20km (12 mile) ring road circles Naples. Rural roads are usually good and are rarely over-crowded. However, inner city driving is a nightmare, to be avoided wherever possible.

By Ferry

Naples has regular ferry connections with Cagliari, Sardinia (Tirrenia ☎ 081-720 1111); Palermo and Milazzo, Sicily (Tirrenia ☎ 081-720 1111; SNAV, ☎ 081-761 2348; SIREMAR, ☎ 081-580 0340) and Tunis (Linee Lauro, ☎ 081-551 3352). For local ferries, *see* **Transport**. The main passenger terminal is Molo Angioino, opposite Piazza Municipio.

Piazza Trieste e Trento, Naples.

Accidents and Breakdowns

In case of breakdown, ☎ 116 and give your location, car registration and make. The **Automobile Club d'Italia** (24hr emergency ☎ 06-4477) will come to the rescue. This will be expensive unless you have reciprocal cover arranged by your national motoring organisation.

In case of an **accident**, place a warning triangle 50m (55yds) behind the car and call the police (☎ 112 or 113). Exchange names, addresses and insurance details with other parties, ask witnesses to remain and give a statement to the police. Make no statement that might imply liability until you have had a chance to clear your head and take advice.
See also **Driving**

Accommodation see p.91

Airports see p.110

Banks

Banks are open Mon-Fri, 8.30am-1pm and for an hour in the afternoon (usually 3-4pm). The exchange booth in the Stazione Centrale stays open daily, 7am-9pm. Not all banks have exchange facilities, queues can be long and a passport or ID is required for all transactions. Most banks now have ATM machines that can be used with either a credit card or your normal cheque guarantee card.

Bicycles

Cycling in Naples would be suicidal and should not be attempted by visitors. However, many locals choose to use mopeds to negotiate the heavy traffic jams in the city. Mopeds are available for hire from **Italrent** (☎ 018-599 1316).

In Sorrento, mopeds are available from **Sorrento**, Corso Italia 210 ☎ 081-878 1386, while bicycles are rented by **Guarracino**, Via Sant'Antonino 19, ☎ 081-878 1728. There are pleasant, but extremely steep, cycle rides around Massa Lubrense.

Books

Many writers have found the Bay

understandably inspiring. Among those who chose to work here were Virgil, Pliny, Petrarch, and Dante. Visiting writers unable to resist a comment include Harriet Beecher Stowe (*Agnes of Sorrento*); Charles Dickens (*Pictures from Italy*); JW Goethe (*Italian Journey*); Alphonse de Lamartine (*Graziella; The Gulf of Baia*); Ivan Turgenev (*A Night in Sorrento*); HV Morton (*A Traveller in Southern Italy*) and Norman Lewis (*Naples '44*).

For background information, start with Valerio (*A Traveller's History of Italy*); Luigi Barzi (*The Italians*); Burton Anderson (*Wines of Italy*); and Valentina Harris (*Valentina's Regional Italian Cookery*).

Camping

There are good camping and caravan sites in the area, although none in Naples itself. The nearest camp site to the city centre is **Volcana Solfatara**, Via Solfatara 16, Pozzuoli, ☎ **081-526 7413**. A full list of options is available from tourist offices or from **Touring Club Italiano** (TCI), Corso Italia 10, Milan, ☎ **02-852 6245**. It is not advisable to drive a caravan along the Amalfi coast road.

Car Hire

Car hire is expensive in Italy, so shop around for a good deal.

Think carefully about whether you need to hire at all, as a car is largely unnecessary in this area.

You must be over 21 (some companies stipulate a minimum age of 23). Most companies have an upper age limit of 60-65. Drivers must have held their full licence for at least a year.

Weekly rates with unlimited mileage offer the best deal; these include breakdown service and basic insurance, but you are advised to take out a collision damage waiver and personal accident insurance in addition. The small local firms generally offer the cheapest rates, but they can only be booked locally. A fly-drive deal or pre-booking may get you a better price. Unless paying by credit card, a substantial cash deposit is required.

All the major car hire companies are represented:

Avis
Airport, ☎ **081-780 5790**
Via Piedigrotta 44, Naples,
☎ **081-761 1365**
Stazione Centrale, Piazza Garibaldi, ☎ **081-554 3020**
Eurodollar
Airport, ☎ **081-780 2963**
Via Partenope 13,
☎ **081-764 6364**
Europcar
Airport, ☎ **081-780 5643**
Via Scarfoglio 10,
☎ **081-570 8426**
Hertz
Airport, ☎ **081-599 0924**

Via Sauro 21, ☎ **081-764 5323**
Piazza Garibaldi 93,
☎ **081-554 8657**
Interrentacar
Via Partenope 37,
☎ **081-764 5060**
Italrent
Airport, ☎ **081-599 1316**
Maggiore
Airport, ☎ **081-780 3011**
Via Cervantes 92,
☎ **081-552 1900**
Stazione Centrale, Piazza
Garibaldi, ☎ **081-287 858**

Children
The Italians are very child
friendly, to the point where
children from less demonstrative
cultures may rebel against being
petted. All hotels welcome
children and most have facilities
such as cots. Nappies, baby food
and other necessities are readily
available. Children under 4 get
free transport and museum
entry; from 4-12, they cost half
price. It is quite common for
children to eat out with their
parents in the evenings.

Churches see Religion

Climate see Weather p.89

Clothing
The Italians dress smartly but not
formally. Any sightseeing trip will
involve a lot of walking, so comfortable shoes are essential.
Sunglasses and a shady hat are
other necessities in summer.
Wear cool clothes, preferably of
natural fabrics, with room for the
air to circulate.

Beach clothes are not acceptable city wear. Topless bathing is
acceptable, nude bathing is not.
If visiting churches, cover your
shoulders and wear long trousers
or a skirt below the knee.

In spring and autumn, the
weather can be changeable, so
work on the layer principle, with
a couple of jumpers and a light
jacket. In winter, you will need a
heavier, rainproof coat.

Men's suits

Italy	46	48	50	52	54	56
UK/US	36	38	40	42	44	46

Men's shirts

Italy	36	37	38	39/40	41	42	43
UK/US	14	14.5	15	15.5	16	16.5	17

Men's shoes

Italy	41	42	43	44	45	46
UK	7	7.5	8.5	9.5	10.5	11
US	8	8.5	9.5	10.5	11.5	12

Women's dresses

Italy	38	40	42	44	46	48
UK	8	10	12	14	16	18
US	6	8	10	12	14	16

Women's shoes

Italy	38	38	39	39	40	41
UK	4.5	5	5.5	6	6.5	7
US	6	6.5	7	7.5	8	8.5

Consulates
UK: Via Francesco Crispi 122,
80122, Naples, ☎ **081-663 511**
Fax: 081-761 3720
USA: Piazza della Repubblica 2,
80122, Naples, ☎ **081-583 8111**

Crime

The high-level corruption and crime for which the city has an unfortunate reputation should not affect tourists. There *is* a high rate of petty crime in certain areas of Naples but visitors should be safe if they follow the same sensible precautions as in any big city. Check change carefully; use a handbag with a zip and shoulder strap slung diagonally; never carry a wallet in a back pocket; and avoid wearing expensive jewellery, cameras, binoculars etc. Avoid the rougher areas of town altogether, and don't walk around alone at night. Keep separate copies of all vital documents.

Currency *see* Money

Customs and Entry Regulations

Italy is part of the European Union and has standard EU customs allowances. Guidelines for goods bought **duty-paid** within the EU are 800 cigarettes, 400 cigarillos, 200 cigars, 10 litres of spirits, 20 litres of fortified wine, 90 litres of wine and 110 litres of beer. For **duty-free goods bought outside the EU**, allowances are: 200 cigarettes or 100 cigarillos or 50 cigars or 250g tobacco; 1 litre of spirits or 2 litres of sparkling or fortified wine and 2 litres of still wine; 50g perfume or 250cc of toilet water.

Street market near Ercolano.

A-Z FACTFINDER

Disabled Visitors

While the Italians are willing to help, facilities are generally poor. The whole area is potentially very difficult for disabled visitors and those requiring wheelchair access, with ultra-steep hills, stepped streets with no vehicular access, cobbles and uneven paving slabs. Plan ahead very carefully.

For information before you travel contact **RADAR** (Royal Association for Disability and Rehabilitation), 12 City Forum, 250 City Road, London EC1V 8AF, ☎ **(0171) 250 3222**, Fax: (0171) 250 1212; or **Holiday Care Service**, 2nd Floor, Imperial Buildings, Victoria Rd, Horley, Surrey RH6 7PZ, ☎ **(01293) 774 535**. In the USA contact **SATH** (Society for the Advancement of Travel for the Handicapped), 347 Fifth Ave, Ste 610, New York NY10016, ☎ **(212) 447 7284**, Fax: (212) 725 8253); or **Mobility International USA**, PO Box 10767, Eugene, Oregon 97440, ☎ **(541) 343 1284**.

Driving

EU drivers may use their national licence; all others need an international driving permit, available through motoring organisations. If driving your own car, you will also need a *Green Card* and it is advisable to take out extended breakdown cover. It is compulsory to keep all relevant papers, including the car ownership documents, in the car at all times.

Drive on the right and give way to traffic coming from the right (although some Italian drivers apparently take no notice of this rule and prefer to use their horns rather than their brakes). Speed limits for normal cars are 50kph (30mph) in built-up areas, 110kph (66mph) on rural roads, and 130kph (80mph) on motorways. Drinking and driving is strictly forbidden, with on-the-spot penalties.

Car parks: Once in Naples, leave your car in your hotel car park or a long-term car park until you are ready to leave, as driving in Naples is to be avoided when possible. There are car parks at: **Parcheggio di interscambio**, Via Benedetto Brin, ☎ **081-763 2832**; **Garage dei Fiori**, Via Colonna 21, ☎ **081-414 190**; **Grilli**, Via Ferrari 40, ☎ **081-264 344**; **Mergellina**, Via Mergellina 112, ☎ **081-761 3470**; **Sannazaro**, Piazza Sannazaro 142, ☎ **081-681 437**; **Santa Chiara**, Pallonetto Santa Chiara 30, ☎ **81-551 6303**; **Supergarage**, Via Shelley 11, ☎ **081-551 3104**; **Turistico**, Via De Gasperi, ☎ **081-552 5442**.

In Naples, there are 24hr service stations at Piazza Carlo III, Via Foria, Piazza Municipio, and Piazza Mergellina. Petrol is

some of the most expensive in Europe, although diesel is slightly cheaper.
See also **Accidents and Breakdowns** and **Car Hire**

Electric Current
The voltage in Italy is usually 220V AC, 50 cycles. Most plugs and sockets are of the two round pin variety, though a few have three round pins. Take a travel adaptor.

Emergencies
General emergency ☎ 113
Police ☎ 112
Fire ☎ 115
Ambulance
    ☎ **081-752 0696** (24 hrs)
    or **081-752 0850** (day only)
Car breakdown ☎ 116
Coastguard ☎ **081-206 118/9**
    or **081-206 133/231**

Excursions see Tours

Guidebooks
see **Maps and Guides**

Health
Italy has good food, clean water and few serious diseases. The quality of medical care is excellent, if the hygiene in the hospitals leaves a little to be desired. There are reciprocal arrangements with all other EU countries, but travel insurance with full medical cover is still advised, and UK nationals should carry a form E111.

Pharmacies (identified by a green cross) are able to assist with many minor ailments and dispense medicines that often need a prescription in other countries. Each town operates a rota for late night and weekend opening. **Farmacia Almasalus**, Piazza Dante 71, ☎ **081-549 9336**, stays open 24hrs a day.

For a **doctor**, ask your hotel, or check the yellow pages under *Unità Sanitaria*. If in doubt, call the **Guardia Medica**, ☎ **081-563 1111**, or go to **Casualty** (*Pronto Soccorso*) at Ospedale Cardarelli, Via Cardarelli 9, ☎ **081-747 2956**; Ospedale dei Pellegrini, Via Portamedina 41, ☎ **081-563 3234**; or Ospedale San Paolo, Via Terracina 219, ☎ **081-768 6284**.

Language
Italian is a rhythmic and beautiful language, easy to learn and speak. Grammar and pronunciation are both logical. Use the polite *lei* (plural) to strangers; the more familiar second person singular, *tu*, is reserved for friends and children.

The 'c' is hard (as in 'cat') when followed by an 'a', 'o', 'u', 'he' or 'hi'. 'c' followed by 'i' or 'e' and 'cc' are both pronounced 'ch' (as in 'church'). 'g' is hard (as in 'go') before 'a', 'o', 'u', 'he' or 'hi', but is softened after 'i' or 'e' (as in 'generous'). If there is an 'h' after 'c' or 'g'

Good morning / Buon giorno
Good afternoon or evening / Buona sera
Good night / Buona notte
Hello/Bye (informal) / Ciao
Goodbye / Arrivederci
Yes / Si
No / No
Please / Per favore
Thank you (very much) / Grazie (molto)
Excuse me (in a crowd) / Permesso
Excuse me / Mi scusi/prego
You're welcome / Prego
Do you speak English? / Parla inglese?
I don't understand / Non capisco
Gentlemen/Ladies / Signori/Signore
Entrance/exit / Entrata/uscita
Arrivals/departures / Arrivi/partenze
No smoking / Vietato fumare
Out of order / Guasto
Where is …? / Dov'è …?
When …? / Quando …?
What is …? / Cos'è …?
How much/many …? / Quanto/quanti …?

(at the beginning or in the middle of a word) the 'c' or 'g' are hard (e.g. *sacchi* or *ghepardo*). 's' is hard ('zz') when used at the beginning of a word, used as a double or followed by another consonant; soft in the middle of a word. 'z' is pronounced 'ts'. A few helpful words and phrases are given above.

Laundry

Most hotels offer a laundry service. Coin-operated launderettes are rare, although *lavanderia* do service washes. There are plenty of dry cleaners in residential areas.

Lost Property

There is no central lost property office. For possessions lost on trains or in stations, contact the **Stazione Centrale**, ☎ 081-567 2927.

Maps and Guides

A full range of maps and guides is published by Michelin. The Michelin sheet map **988** Italy (1/100 000) covers the whole of the country. If you are planning to tour the area, the regional map **431** (1/400 000) will help you to plan your route. The *Michelin Green Guide Italy* includes information on Naples, with detailed descriptions of its principal monuments, museums and other attractions, together with town plans. It also covers the other towns and attractions in the Bay of Naples, the Sorrentine Peninsula and the Amalfi Coast. Information on restaurants and accommodation can be found in the *Michelin Red Guide Italia*, which is updated every year.

Media

Italy has a huge selection of **newspapers and magazines** of which the two most reputable dailies are *La Repubblica* and *Corriere della Sera*. At least one store in each resort sells an array of foreign papers, probably a day old. The Neapolitan daily paper, *Il Mattino*, has good entertainment listings.

There are three official state **TV** channels, several more private, cable and satellite options, all of universally poor quality. Larger hotels offer a variety of satellite channels, including CNN, BBC World Service, Sky, and French and German stations.

There are numerous **radio** stations and some dedicated searching should find one to match your personal taste.

Money

The Italian lire is now linked to the Euro and is steady at about 2 800 lire to UK£1 and 1850 lire to US$1. It will vanish, along with many other European currencies in 2001. Notes come in denominations of 1 000, 2 000, 5 000, 10 000, 50 000 and 100 000 (also 500 000, which fortunately are only delivered by banks) lire. Coins come in denominations of 50, 100, 200, 500 and 1 000 lire. The huge numbers of noughts can cause confusion, so learn your notes and check change carefully.

All major credit cards are widely accepted. Eurocheques are not recommended. *See also* **Banks**

Opening Hours

Banks: Mon-Fri 8.30am-1pm and for 1 hr in the afternoon (usually 3-4pm).
Post Offices: main offices Mon-Sat 8.30am-7.30pm; smaller branches usually open Mon-Fri 8.30am-5pm, Sat 8.30am-noon.
Shops: Mon-Sat 8/9am-1pm, 4-7/8pm. More are now opening on Sundays.

Museums and sights: hours vary but museums usually open in the mornings and are closed all day Monday. The main churches may be open all day but some close in the afternoons.

Tourist Offices: hours vary but standard times are generally Mon-Sat 9am-1pm, 4-7pm.

Photography

Film of all types is freely available, as are facilities for getting photos developed. The midday light is very harsh, so serious photographers should take a range of film speeds and a UV filter.

It is illegal to photograph any military installation and inside many museums. Those that do allow photography still forbid flash.

Police

The *vigili urbani* (town police) are mainly concerned with traffic and parking offences. The *polizia stradale* fulfil the same function on the motorways and outside towns. The *carabinieri* handle most general crime, but thefts should be reported to the *polizia statale*.

Police Headquarters are at Via Medina 75, ☎ **081-794 1111**.

Post Offices

There is at least one post office in each town, but stamps (*francobolli*) are also available from many hotels, newsagents and tobacconists which display a blue sign with a white 'T'. *Poste restante* (in Italian: *Fermo posta*) facilities are available at most post offices, but there is a small

Ferry leaving the island of Ischia.

charge for collecting mail.
See also **Opening Hours**

Public Holidays

1 January: New Year's Day
6 January: Epiphany
Easter Day and Easter Monday
25 April: Liberation Day
1 May: Labour Day
15 August: Assumption of the
   Virgin
1 November: All Saints' Day
8 December: Immaculate
   Conception
25 December: Christmas Day
26 December: Boxing Day
   Many towns also add their own
holidays, based on the feast days
of their patron saints.

Religion

Italy is a Roman Catholic
country and mass is celebrated
in Italian in most churches every
Sunday. There are Catholic
churches around every corner.
Naples is sufficiently cosmopoli-
tan to have representatives of
most branches of Christianity
and other major faiths, including
Judaism, Islam and Hinduism.
Complete listings are given in
Qui Napoli, available free from
tourist offices.

Smoking

The number of people who
smoke is significantly higher
than in the UK or USA and there
are virtually no areas set aside for
non-smokers, even in many
restaurants. Smoking is, however,
banned in museums, art galleries
and churches, and there are
separate non-smoking compart-
ments in trains.

Telephones

The Italian telephone system is
good but there are not as many
public phone boxes as might be
expected. Most public phones
take either credit cards or phone
cards to the value of 5 000,
10 000 and 15 000 lire (*schede
telefoniche*), sold at newsagents
and tobacconists. Coin-operated
booths use 100, 200 or 500 lire
coins, or more rarely 200 lire
tokens (*gettoni*). For international calls, use a phone booth
(*telefono a scatti*) where you speak
first then pay for the call, available in some bars, hotels and
post offices.

   There are plenty of direct
access opportunities, with most
international phone cards,
'Country Direct' numbers and
GSM mobile phones recognised.
Tariffs are cheapest between
10pm-8am Monday to Saturday,
and all day Sunday.
To call Italy from abroad,
   ☎ **00 39**
Area code for Naples, ☎ **081**
Operator, ☎ **15**
International operator
   (Intercontinental), ☎ **170**
Local directory enquiries, ☎ **12**
International directory
   enquiries, ☎ **176**

Reverse charge calls, ☎ 172, followed by the country code
Country codes are as follows:
Australia ☎ 00 61
Canada ☎ 00 1
Ireland ☎ 00 353
New Zealand ☎ 00 64
UK ☎ 00 44
USA ☎ 00 1

Time

Italian standard time is one hour ahead of GMT. Italian Summer Time (IST) begins on the last weekend in March when the clocks go forward an hour (the same day as British Summer Time), and ends on the last weekend in September when the clocks go back (one month before BST ends). New York is 6hrs behind Italy; Sydney is 8hrs ahead.

Tipping

Hotel staff: about 1-2 000 lire for the porter, doorman or room service. About the same, per day, for the chambermaid.
Restaurants: there is usually a 10-15 per cent service charge included in the bill, but it is customary to leave some small change as well.
Taxis: about 10 per cent.
Bars: a small tip up-front assures better service.
Theatres: ushers normally expect a small tip for showing you to your seat.
Churches and other sights:

a custodian who opens a locked area for you will expect a small gratuity.

Toilets

Museums, sights, stations, bars and restaurants all have good public toilets. Beyond this, they are rare and generally unpleasant. Carry your own supply of tissues. If there is an attendant, tip about 200 lire.

Tourist Information Offices

The **Italian State Tourist Office** (ENIT) is a good initial source of information about the city or region you are visiting, including accommodation, travel and places of interest (website: www.enit.it). It has offices in the following English-speaking countries:
Canada: 1 Place Ville Marie Ste 1914, Quebec H3B 3M9, Montreal, ☎ 514- 866 0975/514-866 7667/8/9 Fax: 514-392 1429 E-mail: initaly@ican.net
UK: 1 Princess St, London W1R 8AY, ☎ 0171-408 1254 Fax: 0171-493 6695 E-mail: enitlond@globalnet.co.uk
USA: 630 Fifth Ave, Ste 1565, New York 10111, NY, ☎ 212-245 4822 Fax: 212-586 9249

Italy is divided into 20 regions, each with a Regional Tourist Board. The regions are further divided into provinces, each with a provincial capital which has a tourist board, called **Ente**

Provinciale Turismo (EPT). The Provincial Tourist Office is in Naples at Piazza dei Martiri 58, Naples 80121, ☎ 081-405 311, Fax: 081-401 961. There are also kiosks at: **Stazione Mergellina**, ☎ 081-761 2102; **Aeroporto Capodichino**, ☎ 081-780 5761; and **Stazione Centrale FS**, ☎ 081-268 779.

There are local tourist board offices (**Azienda Promozione Turistica/APT**) in the following towns:

Naples
City Tourist Information, Via Plebiscito, Palazzo Reale, ☎ 081-418744 Fax: 081-418 619 Information Office, Piazza del Gesù Nuovo 7, ☎ 081-552 3328 Fax: 081-551 2701; and Piazza dei Martiri 58, ☎ 081-405 311.

A toll-free helpline, *Hello Napoli* is on ☎ 167-251 396 (information in Italian, English, French and German).

Pozzuoli
Via Campi Flegrei 3, ☎ 081-526 2419 Fax: 081-526 1481 Piazza Matteotti 1/a, ☎ 081-526 6639

Pompeii
Via Sacra 1, ☎ 081-850 7255 Fax: 081-863 2401

Capri
Head Office
Piazzetta I, Cerio 11, ☎ 081-837 5308 Fax: 081-837 0918
Information Offices
Capri
Piazza Umberto I, ☎ 081-837-

0686
Marina Grande
Banchina del Porto, ☎ 081-837 0634
Anacapri
Via G. Orlandi, 59, ☎ 081-837 1524
Ischia
Stazione Marittima, Ischia di Porto, ☎ 081-991 146
Ischia e Procida
Corso Vittorio Colonna 116, Ischia di Porto, ☎ 081-991 464 Fax: 081-981 904
Procida
Via Marina, ☎ 081-810 1968
Sorrento
Circolo dei Forestieri (Foreigners' Club), Via L. De Maio 35, ☎ 081-807 4033 Fax: 081-877 3397. Open Mon-Sat 8.30am-2.30pm, 3.30-6.30pm
Castellamare di Stabia
Piazza Matteotti 34/35, ☎ 081-871 1334
Positano
Via Saracino 4, ☎ 089-875 067 Fax: 089-875 760
Amalfi
Corso delle Repubbliche Marinare 27, ☎ 089-871 107 Fax: 089-872 619
Ravello
Piazza Duomo 10, ☎ 089-857 096 Fax: 089-857 977

Tours
Naples: The Chamber of Commerce organises a programme of free city and area tours, with pickups from various

hotels and key points, and commentaries in Italian, English, French and German. Pick up a brochure and complimentary tickets from travel agents and hotels.

Taxi tours are offered by **Consortaxi** (Piazza S. Maria La Nova 44, ☎ 081-552 0205; Numero Verde: 1670-16221), including tourist itineraries in and around Naples, and excursions to Pompeii, Herculaneum, Sorrento and the Amalfi Coast, by taxi. Bookable direct or through hotels.

Sorrento: For information on local tours, contact the **Guide Centre** (Via degli Aranci 187, Sorrento, ☎ 081-878 3061, Fax: 081-877 2197). One call to this superb facility will provide you with a highly knowledgeable tour guide to conduct you around anywhere in the Bay of Naples area. Over a dozen languages available.

Transport

Tickets: *Giranapoli* tickets, on sale at all stations and most tobacconists and newsagents, are valid on all buses, metros, funiculars and trams in the Naples metropolitan area. At the time of writing, they cost 1 500 lire for 90 mins travelling time; 4 500 lire for a full day. Buy ahead and simply date-stamp the tickets to validate them the first time you use them. There are machines on board all buses, trams and trains. There are frequent ticket inspections, with instant fines.

The **Tourist Card** (30 000 lire from the airport, railway stations, ports, and hotels and travel agencies displaying the sign QUI) offers 48 hours of unlimited metropolitan transport and 10 days of discounts on ferry tickets to the islands, museums, restaurants and participating shops.

Bus/coach

Locals complain bitterly about the buses in **Naples**, but the service is excellent, traffic jams permitting, with a wide network of numbered orange buses. A bus map is available from the tourist office. Main hubs include Piazza Garibaldi, Piazza Trieste e Trente, and Piazza della Repubblica. An elderly **tram** also trundles along the seafront.

For travelling by coach around the region, the main local coach operators include:

ACTP, Via Arenaccia 29, Naples, ☎ 081-700 1111. Local services to the Vesuvius area and Caserta; departing from Piazza Capuana, near Piazza Garibaldi.

SEPSA, Via Cisterna dell'Olio 44, Naples, ☎ 081-735 4197. Services to the Campi Flegrei; leaving from Piazza Garibaldi.

SITA, Via Pisanelli 3-7, Naples, ☎ 081-552 2176. Local services to the Sorrentine Peninsula and

Amalfi Coast; departing from the office in Via Pisanelli, near Piazza Municipio.

Metro
At present, the Naples metro has only two lines, one an interlinking rail service between the main FS stations, the other heading north through Vomero. Neither is of much use to tourists. A new line is under construction, but work has been going on for years with little sign of progress.

Funicular
Four fast, frequent and reliable funiculars climb the steep hills behind the city centre. Three – from Via del Parco Margherita, near Piazza Amedeo; from Via Toledo, near Piazza Trieste e Trento; and from Piazza Montesanto, a few blocks from Piazza Dante – converge on Vomero. The fourth, from Via Mergellina, climbs through the district of Mergellina to the west.

Taxis
Taxis are expensive, with numerous additions to the metered fare, according to time of day, amount of luggage, destination (the airport costs more) etc. Meters are often mysteriously broken, roads seem to be three times as long as normal, and so on, so keep a watchful eye on the price.
Radio Taxis in Naples:
Partenope ☎ 081-560 6666/556 0202
Napoli ☎ 081-556 4444

Three-wheeler taxis on Ischia.

Free ☎ 081-551 5151
Cotana ☎ 081-570 7070
Taxis in Sorrento:
Sorrento ☎ 081-878 2204
Sant'Agnello ☎ 081-878 1428

Limousine Services
American Limousine Service,
Via Manzoni 141/c, Naples,
☎ 081-575 5880
Syrenbus, Sorrento, ☎ 081-807 4220.
Luxury limousine service for
transfers and full and half day
sightseeing. Prices are not too
astronomical if several
passengers share.

Ferry
An excellent network of hydro-
foils and ferries connects Naples,
Sorrento, Capri, Ischia, Procida
and Pozzuoli, with occasional
services round to Positano and
Amalfi.
*Hydrofoil/ferry services from Molo
Beverello:*
Caremar ☎ 081-551 3882
Naples to Capri, Ischia and
Procida
NLG ☎ 081-552 7209
Naples to Capri
Alilauro ☎ 081-552 2838
Naples to Sorrento, Ischia
Hydrofoil services from Mergellina:
Alilauro ☎ 081-761 1004
Naples to Ischia
SNAV ☎ 081-761 2348
Naples to Capri, Casamicciola,
and Procida

Train
The **Circumvesuviana** line
operates frequent services from
Naples to Ercolano, Pompeii and
Sorrento, from a station on
Corso Garibaldi, about 200m
(220yds) from the Stazione
Centrale. For enquiries,
☎ numero verde 1478-88088.
   The **Ferrovia Cumana** and the
Circumflegrea take different
routes through the western
suburbs of Naples to meet up
again at Torregaveta. Both leave
from Piazza Montesanto, ☎ 081-551 3328.

Vaccinations
see **Before You Go, p.110**

Water
The tap water is perfectly safe to
drink, but most people, including the Italians, prefer to drink
bottled mineral water, which is
readily available.

Youth Hostels
see **Accommodation, p.91**

INDEX